How to be with God:
a primer on Christian prayer

How to be with God: a Primer on Christian Prayer

Published in association with Westwinds Community Church,
1000 Robinson Road, Jackson, MI 49203. www.westwinds.org.

Edited by Amy Gafkjen.

Book design by Mel Evans.

TABLE OF CONTENTS

For my father, Gordon Arthur McDonald.
Thank you for showing me God is good,
and that I can be, too.

GOD LIKES MY JOKES

I pray that the eyes of your heart may be enlightened ...
- St. Paul, Letter to the Church in Ephesus

I feel the same way about people who love prayer
as I do about people who love conversation: they're
missing the point. I only enjoy *some* conversation, like
with people I appreciate or might begin to love. Other
conversations can be dreadful.

"Prayer" is a thing I don't like. But God? Him, I love.

I do not want you to love prayer, since, as Abraham
Heschel said, "The issue of prayer is not prayer; the
issue of prayer is God."[1] I want you to experience the
slow burn of God's love as it intensifies over time; but,
in order for you to better experience God's love, you're
probably going to have to pray.

Unfortunately, it's tough to pray when you feel like
trash. Or worse. And the very fact that we're not
praying more makes most of us feel terrible. Our guilt
about not praying keeps us from prayer, and the cycle
perpetuates.

This book is designed to help you feel empowered
and inspired to pray. I want you to enjoy prayer, on
your own terms, without any need to justify how or
when or why you pray. Because, once you begin, it's

wonderful. It's easy. Like being with an old friend. Like catching up. Like getting advice from someone you admire.

I often laugh while praying because I think God likes my jokes. I imagine he's excited when I call because he enjoys the spin I put on my stories. He knows the punchlines, of course, but the greatness of a story is in the *telling*. He's a brilliant audience. He hangs on every word. After, he's always got feedback for me— on the performance, on the set-up, the writing, and the issues backstage. His critiques are spot on, and I'm glad whenever I make the recommended change.

Have I gone too far afield? Does this no longer sound like prayer?

Good. Because this isn't a book for people who already know how prayer is supposed to be. This is for everyone who wants to know if prayer can be anything other than a prison sentence, or if prayer still counts when you muff it up.

I'll teach you how to pray, but it'll have to be you that does the praying. My prayers out of your mouth are going to feel angular, so you'll have to hum the tune until you write new words.

Prayer is the most honest thing about us. We only really pray when we've got nowhere else to aim our anger or chuck our tears or shout our frustration. Prayer is the only place we are truly loved.

Prayer is like children's artwork on God's fridge. Prayer is the poem you wrote when you proposed, the tender intricacy of a long and healthy romance. Prayer is the first time you made someone proud, and the moment you forgave an old wound.

> It is as though God has a favorite food. When we pray, he smells the aroma from the kitchen as you prepare his special dish. When God hungers for some special satisfaction he seeks out a prayer to answer. Our prayer is the sweet aroma from the kitchen ascending up into the King's chambers making him hungry for the meal. But the actual enjoyment of the meal is his own glorious work in answering our prayers.
> - John Piper[2]

Though I'm reluctant to categorize, it is fair to say there are two broad kinds of spiritual people: actives and contemplatives. Most people think the contemplatives are the spiritual ones (they like silence and solitude and vigils and saints). But being spiritual is an abstract concept. The Bible speaks far more about being healthy than it does about being transcendent, so our goal ought to be purity rather than profundity.

A perfectly healthy bear will never be tender like a perfectly healthy kitten. God made you to be perfectly you. So don't stress about being spiritual. Be you, purified—the best possible version of you for the glory of God. If you're contemplative, be purely contemplative. But if you're active, be perfectly active. Roam. Romp. Bellow. Rant. Roar.

God wants lions as much as lambs.

> Prayer is translation. A man translates himself into a child asking for all there is in a language he has barely mastered.
> - Leonard Cohen[3]

This book is divided into ten chapters, each addressing a common concern about prayer. Don't worry. I'll still answer the big one: *Why won't God do what I want?* And its cousins: *Is God even listening?* and *What's the point?*

I've included several exercises at the end of each chapter, along with a short introduction to **famous pray-ers** and a suggestion on how to pray like them. I've included these exercises to help you know what to say when you can't figure out what to say on your own. Having a format to guide us through prayer is an easy way to avoid being dumbstruck when we spend focused time with God.

The best understanding of prayer is constant conversation with God throughout the day. Properly understood, and when consciously wrangled toward heaven, even our thoughts are prayers. This isn't automatically the case, but with practice it is possible to be continuously in prayer (see 1 Thessalonians 5.16-18). Nevertheless, it is still important to set aside time exclusively for prayer. To distinguish between the constant prayers of faithful Christians and exclusively-prayer times, I will refer to the latter as "focused" time with God. "Focused time with God" is when you're by yourself, with no distractions, earnestly seeking Christ. I've also taken to using the term pray-ers in reference to those that pray. Of course "Christians" would suffice, but many Christians don't consider themselves competent pray-ers, and the simple adaptation of this otherwise normal term slows us down and helps us consider how God might be maturing us through conversation with him.

Also, I imagine the two kinds of pray-ers will each need suggestions about how to move forward, so I've provided **exercises for actives and contemplatives** at the end of each chapter. Feel free to change them, adapt them, or ignore them. Likewise, I've given a HACK for how to pray along a certain style. Whereas the exercises are kinesthetic activities, the HACKS are mental rubrics for guiding what you say or think.

One essential skill I'd like to highlight here is **learning to pray the Bible**. I suggest you read passages from God's Word and make them your own, repurposed as prayer. It makes for good conversation and provides the added bonus of ensuring your thinking is sound.

Every book has goals. Mine are simple. I want you to experience more of God and less of your guilt; greater comfort and less condemnation; so prayer becomes a way of life, rather than a departure from it.

I want you to live comfortably with God.

Let's begin to learn how …

WE
LEARN
TO
PRAY
BY
PRAYING

Prayer cannot be taught; it can only be done.
- A.W. Tozer[4]

Prayer is like falling off a bike. Everyone teases that we'll get it right eventually, but in the moment prayer is an invitation to scrape your knees and ugly-cry.

I've read so much about prayer. I've tried every kind of praying imaginable, and I've come to hate everything about prayer except praying. And just like no one can teach you how to be in love, no one can teach you how to be in prayer.

We learn to pray by praying.

Ronald Rolheiser, my favorite contemporary spiritual writer, advises us to "show up for prayer, and show up regularly."[5] Take the leap. Dip your toe. Close your eyes. Hold your breath. In so doing, we educate our intuitions concerning how we best experience God's presence.

Everyone prays differently. When they don't, it's probably not their prayer they're praying. They're aping someone else. That's ok. There's no copyright on piety. But I don't want you to feel like you're doing it wrong.

I confess, I pray like I do everything else—I wing it.

Other people have always made me feel guilty about prayer. Sometimes intentionally, but mostly I felt guilty because they were better at it than I was. Or enjoyed it more. Or faked both sufficiently well that I felt like the lone pagan at the Easter vigil.

There was an elderly man from Hong Kong who used to attend my boyhood church. He read the entire Bible every thirty days, cover to cover. He also prayed for eight hours a day on a wooden stool he'd made in his shed. Kneeling stools are very popular in Asia, and his was so well-used there were divots where his knees had rested. His knees has callouses. The only other people I know with callouses on their knees lay floor tile for a living. His living was prayer.

This senior saint told me prayer was the key to faith, and faith was the key to pleasing God. He was a powerful man, so I tried to pray like him but couldn't get anywhere close. For several weeks I even set my alarm clock for 4 a.m. to get in a few extra hours before school.

Why didn't I realize sooner that the man was retired? That he had no family, no hobbies, nowhere to go, and nothing to do? He was one step removed from a nursing home, and I was trying to match my schedule to his. If the reverse had occurred, he'd have split his colostomy and died of sepsis on the first day.

When I was in college I attended Tuesday morning prayer meetings at 6 a.m. I hated them. I dragged myself there, under protest, and spent an hour asking God to forgive me for my resentment. The gathering was held by a consortium of cheerful retirees who all went to breakfast afterwards. It was years before

I learned that they naturally woke up at 5 a.m. every day, took midmorning naps, and went to sleep at dusk after *Matlock*. They used to poke me for being tired and lecture me on my responsibilities to be faithful in prayer. But I was newly married. I was working two jobs. I was a collegiate athlete on a scholarship, and I was running a major ministry in my local church. Why didn't they just tell me "good job" and let me sleep? Why did they sell me water at a high price, right next to the river?[6]

That idealized concept of prayer only ever resulted in my condemnation—from the old men, from myself, and from others who felt like the old men had it right.

Comparisons are no more helpful than watching someone else eat. You see what they do, and you see how they feel, but that does nothing to alleviate the twist of your gut or the thickness of your tongue.

The good news is that I don't think about those old men any longer. I had to pick at that scab to illustrate that other people will set up rules if you let them. So don't let them. Prayer isn't about impressing them, or being one of them, or even agreeing with them. Prayer is about you and God living comfortably together. If you're miserable when you pray, so is God. Miserable prayer is like an awkward dinner date before you muster the courage to break off a courtship.

Stop prolonging your agony.

Pray in such a way that you enjoy it. Because, if you'll find a way to make it work, God will accommodate. This, I think, is what Brother Lawrence meant when he said, "Neither skill nor knowledge is needed to go to God, but only a heart determined to devote itself to Him."[7]

> I prayed like a man walking in a forest at night, feeling his way with his hands, at each step fearing to fall into pure bottomlessness forever. Prayer is like lying awake at night, afraid, with your head under the cover, hearing only the beating of your own heart.
> - Wendell Berry[8]

It's worth mentioning there are few instructions in the Bible about how to pray.

- We're told, for instance, that we should pray (see Philippians 4.6; Mark 11.24; Luke 11.9; 1 Timothy 2.1-4; Ephesians 6.18; etc.).
- We're also told to whom we should pray (to the Father, through the Son, by the Holy Spirit—see Matthew 6.9; Romans 8.26).
- We're also told that we should praise God (see Ephesians 5.20; 1 Chronicles 16.8), thank God (see Colossians 4.2; Psalm 34.1), and beseech God (see Matthew 21.22; John 16.24).

But apart from Jesus' instruction in Matthew 6 concerning the Lord's Prayer and St. Paul's instructions in 1 Thessalonians 5 to pray without ceasing, we're never told *how*.

So let's begin with the obvious question: How did Jesus pray?

I once asked my friend Lori Wagner for insight on this issue. Lori is an exceptional researcher and I consider her an expert in Second Temple Judaism. She helped me put things in perspective, focusing on Jesus' life as a first century Jew.

Since Jesus was from Galilee—a more conservative, devout portion of Judea—he would have followed the rituals of a faithful Jewish male. Those would have included prayers in the morning and evening, at meals, as well as frequent blessings whenever the occasion permitted. We know Jesus based the prayer he taught his disciples[9] on some common prayers, which was typical for rabbis.

We know Jesus prayed to his "Father," which is more intimate than most and must also be understood as a call to be apprenticed in the ways of holiness, since vocation was inherent in the father-son relationships of Judea. And we know Jesus went to places alone to pray frequently, particularly in the morning and evening. He also fasted in preparation for his ministry, enduring forty days without food in emulation of (and recapitulation for) Israel's 40 years of wandering in the desert.

Jesus studied and memorized scripture, especially the prophets, and some of what he quoted was non-canonical.[10] Most every quote he made was a paraphrase, which was typical of the time, given that the scriptures were learned in Hebrew but most spoke Aramaic, and translations often varied.

Jesus had such a strong understanding of Jewish regulations that he disputed them with the best authorities on the subject and prevailed. Likewise, he observed all feasts and festivals, including the Festival of Dedication, which was not required by Law but considered authoritative among traditional Jews. These were all occasions of public prayer, and Jesus typically participated with both his family and his disciples, showing that he expected those closest to him not to eschew their social responsibility.

So what can we learn from Jesus' life about how to pray? Simply this: that he was saturated with it, in a variety of forms and on a multitude of occasions. He was never not praying.

> I have prayed for you, that your faith may not
> fail ...
> - Jesus, in Luke 22.32

My parents taught me to pray. First, that I should; then, they taught me how. I recommend you follow suit, as I have, in partial fulfillment of the proverb that advises us to "Start children off on the way they should go, and even when they are old they will not turn from it."[11] Teach your children that prayer is like breathing, that our lungs move the Spirit of God in grace. Teach them to pray before meals because such ordinary prayer allows their confidence to grow as they approach God.

Many children learn how to pray from their parents. Others learn how to pray by listening to their pastors. Most of us just trip our way forward until we finally have the courage to admit we don't know how to get started. But for me, I love the idea that we can learn how to pray best at home. There's something powerful about a praying mother, or a devoted father, or a mom and dad who, together, lead their home in the way of the Lord.

Prayer is only hard for you. And me. But praying isn't hard at all. It's the gap between not praying and starting to pray that's the killer. Once you begin, your first stuttered pleas accelerate into the babble of needs-assistance. And whether you're most comfortable praying in your car or walking in the woods, on your knees or with a cup of joe, there is one inescapable truth about prayer: Prayer changes you. You don't feel any different—except, maybe, stupider—but you're metamorphosing.

Prayer is making you a saint.

TERESA OF AVILA
SPAIN
1515-1582

Mental prayer, in my opinion, is nothing else than an intimate sharing between friends; it means taking time alone with Him who we know loves us. The important thing is not to think much, but to love much, and so do that which best stirs you to love. Love is not great delight, but desire to please God in everything.
- Teresa of Avila[12]

I've got a soft spot for bad girls, and though it may seem strange to say it, this Carmelite nun was full of mischief and charm. I won't belabor Teresa's biography, but let it suffice to say she broke hearts as well as she prayed. And she was a Doctor of Prayer, one of only two women to be so named by the Catholic Church.

Teresa's concept of prayer involved levels of maturation and development. Here's an overview of her philosophy, likened to a garden:

- The first stage is like trying to **draw water from a well** by our own effort. It's slow. It's painful. Sometimes there's no water in the well

24

and we have to wait for it to refill. We must to accept this.

- The second stage, continuing the garden metaphor, involves **drawing water with a hand pump**. There's still strain, but the burden is lessened because we have help. With increased ease comes an increased peace, so that our desires are less intense and we suffer from fewer distractions.

- The third stage occurs when **the entire garden has been irrigated**. Now we don't bother drawing water, but work in the garden next to Christ. We get a sense of perspective, and of progress, as we see what God is making of us.

- The final stage occurs when **the rains come evenly** and water the garden without any human effort at all. We make no effort. Everything grows without strain. There is a pure pleasure of being in the garden with nothing to do but appreciate the beauty of Christ.

If you want to pray like Teresa, first locate yourself in these stages of prayer. Then visualize your prayers as water being brought into the garden of divine love.

**DID YOU
TEST THE
EXERCISE?**

Yes!

No.

**WAS IT
HELPFUL?**

Yes!

No.

Partly...

**WOULD YOU
REPEAT IT?**

Yes!

No.

Notes:

ACTIVE PRAYER
EXERCISE

Active pray-ers are people who like to *do* things, rather than just sit around and *think* things. So the easiest way to begin is to stand up and face the east in the morning or the west in the evening (hint: if you're unsure of the compass, look for the sun).

Many biblical characters prayed this way, including the prophet Daniel.[13] There's nothing magical or scientific about facing east, it's just a simple exercise that'll help get you on your feet and incorporate your body into conversation with God. Simply put, it gives you something to do, and somewhere to go, and something to consider so you feel like you prayed.

Try this for the next seven days. You might miss one or two, so aim for seven and be happy with five.

DID YOU TEST THE EXERCISE?

Yes!

No.

WAS IT HELPFUL?

Yes!

No.

Partly...

WOULD YOU REPEAT IT?

Yes!

No.

Notes:

CONTEMPLATIVE PRAYER
EXERCISE

Contemplative pray-ers enjoy losing themselves in the experience of God. As such, many traditions have crafted prayers that are meant to be repeated over and over, so that the person praying loses focus on the words and gets caught up in the moment. Along with those repeated prayers, many Christians have found it helpful to loosely keep track of the number of times they've prayed them. This, actually, is the origin of prayer beads, which I liken to the fidget cubes of the ancient world.

I suggest praying the Jonah's Prayer ten times while holding onto a string of beads. Every time you complete the prayer, move to the next bead on the string. Pay attention to how you feel and how your thoughts begin to still.

> In my distress I called to the Lord,
>   and he answered me.
> From deep in the realm of the dead I called for help,
>   and you listened to my cry.
> You hurled me into the depths,
>   into the very heart of the seas,
>   and the currents swirled about me;
> all your waves and breakers
>   swept over me.

I said, 'I have been banished
    from your sight;
yet I will look again
    toward your holy temple.'
The engulfing waters threatened me,
    the deep surrounded me;
    seaweed was wrapped around my head.
To the roots of the mountains I sank down;
    the earth beneath barred me in forever.
But you, Lord my God,
    brought my life up from the pit.
When my life was ebbing away,
    I remembered you, Lord,
and my prayer rose to you,
    to your holy temple.
Those who cling to worthless idols
    turn away from God's love for them.
But I, with shouts of grateful praise,
    will sacrifice to you.
What I have vowed I will make good.
    I will say, 'Salvation comes from the Lord.'
- Jonah 2.2-9, NIV

HACK

THE PRAYER HAND[14]

The Navigators is a Christian organization that disciples college students. Their HACK involves associating an aspect of prayer with each digit on your hand. I've outlined it here and suggest you begin by spending two minutes with each "finger" before moving on to the next:

Our little finger represents **confession**—We agree with God about our sin (1 John 1.9: "If we confess our sins, he is faithful and just and will forgive us our sins and purify us from all unrighteousness.").

Our ring finger represents **petition**—We ask God to provide for our needs (1 Samuel 1.27: "I prayed for this child, and the Lord has granted me what I asked of him.").

Our middle finger represents **intercession**—We ask God to provide for the needs of others (Ephesians 6.19: "Pray also for me, that whenever I speak, words may be given me so that I will fearlessly make known the mystery of the gospel …").

Our index finger represents **thanksgiving**—
We thank God for what He has done in,
through, and for us (Ephesians 5.20: "...
always giving thanks to God the Father for
everything, in the name of our Lord Jesus
Christ.").

Our thumb represents **praise**—We let our
enjoyment of God overflow into words. And,
since the thumb is able to touch all four other
fingers, it's worth noting that praise should
permeate every part of our lives (Psalm 146.1-
2: "Praise the Lord. Praise the Lord, my soul.
I will praise the Lord all my life; I will sing
praise to my God as long as I live.").

THE PRAYER HAND

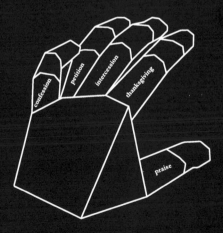

PRAYING THE SCRIPTURES

DANIEL 9

Since we mentioned Daniel in the suggested exercise for actives, let's begin by parsing one of his prayers into our own. This is an excerpt of a much longer prayer, but it's my favorite portion and a good starting place for beginners.

> Now, our God, hear the prayers and petitions of your servant. For your sake, Lord, look with favor on your desolate sanctuary. Give ear, our God, and hear; open your eyes and see the desolation of the city that bears your Name. We do not make requests of you because we are righteous, but because of your great mercy. Lord, listen! Lord, forgive! Lord, hear and act! For your sake, my God, do not delay, because your city and your people bear your Name.
> **Daniel 9.17-19, NIV**

Here's how I would pray this:

> *God—I'm coming back to you, again, doing everything I can to make you proud. But our world is messed up, and I think people are starting to notice. What's worse is that, because they identify you as Creator, they're starting to wonder if maybe you're asleep at the wheel.*

Please help me figure out how best to move forward.
Give me wisdom and strength. Help me proceed
in such a way that I don't do any damage to your
reputation.

I'm asking because you're good, not because I am;
and I have a feeling that your goodness spills over and
benefits everybody else. So please overflow.

Please help. Please listen. Please forgive me for the
stupidity I contributed to this mess in the first place.

And if you could hurry, I'd sure appreciate it.

Amen.

YOUR PRAYER:

DATE:

PRAYER
MAKES
US
SAINTS

> *I came from Latin America where intellectuals were*
> *always talking about political and social revolution*
> *and where a lot of bombs were thrown. But revolution*
> *hasn't changed much. It takes little daring to bomb*
> *a building, but in order to give up cigarettes or stop*
> *being anxious or stop internal chattering, you have to*
> *remake yourself. That is where real reform begins.*
> *- Carlos Castaneda, Peruvian-American mystic[15]*

In prayer, we come to our Father saying, "This is all I've got, unless you make it better."

Prayer is the inoculation against spiritual disease. When we pray, our souls fight the infections of bitterness, victimization, fear, anxiety, and prejudice.

Prayer changes us. Prayer heals us. Prayer grows us. Prayer cures us.

Do you see why we've been so often disappointed with prayer? We keep thinking prayer will heal the world, but when we spend time with God, he wants to heal us first.

Is that too much nonsense? Too vague and spiritual sounding? I hope not. It's the best I can do. It's the closest I can come to helping you understand that your desires and passions and humors are not infections God is wary of contracting. God made you like this— as you!—because he wanted you for himself. You are his. When you pray, God gets his favorite person back.

Prayer is God's cure for acute loneliness, and also his inoculation against such loneliness in the future.

When we pray, God helps us become the best possible version of ourselves. God purifies us, freeing us from all that we carry around as we try to impress others. Prayer keeps us from hiding who we really are and helps us shine instead. Prayer is how we mature into the people God intends us to become.

Prayer is the means by which we consciously and actively become the people we already are, potentially and secretly.

> I have been driven many times upon my knees by the overwhelming conviction that I had nowhere else to go. My own wisdom and that of all about me seemed insufficient for that day.
> - Abraham Lincoln[16]

If we are well-educated, have sufficient income, a loving family, and a sense of optimism for the future … in short, if life is perfect, we may wonder why we bother to pray at all.

Truthfully, no one *needs* to pray.

Prayer is not designed to rewire our brain and make us more skippy. Neither is prayer some strange form of religious mind control, wherein God forces us to become supernatural codependents, needing tireless affirmation from our narcissistic space-papa.

We pray because we want God. We pray because it's good, because it's formative, because it's meaningful. To say that prayer is helpful isn't to suggest that we will receive precisely the kind of help previously specified in conversation with God. Instead, we acknowledge that somehow, with God, everything will be resolved into something better than where it began.

How?
  Who knows?

When?
  Who can tell?

Does God even know?
  Would we be able to tell if he did not?

We're commanded to pray because prayer is less about getting results than becoming tethered to our Creator, slowly metamorphosing us into saints.

> The Lord is near to all those who call on him ...
> - Psalm 145.18, NIV

The essence of prayer is the slow change from being with God to belonging within God. Prayer is how we become God's, because prayer is the best way to know God—not about God, but to know God as he is. Prayer is the vehicle for our relationship with God.

I'm very close with my father, Gordon. We speak together several times a week. I don't often ask him for things. We just stay in touch because we both enjoy it. I get comfort and strength from him, sometimes he tells me I'm misguided, and if I'm in town he sometimes lets me drive his convertible. When Carmel and I were younger and struggling financially, he would sometimes give us cash.

Can you imagine how unpleasant my relationship with my father would be if I only ever called to ask him for money? Or advice? Or to talk endlessly without giving him any opportunity to respond? Yet we do this with God, and somehow imagine that God is the one to blame for the tension in our relationship. But God's character isn't the problem. Our selfish behavior malforms our prayers into tirades. Before we can proceed to know God more deeply we must give him the courtesy of allowing him to respond.

> Every sin is the distortion of an energy breathed into us—an energy which, if not thus distorted, would have blossomed into one of those holy acts whereof "God did it" and "I did it" are both true descriptions. We poison the wine as he decants it into us; murder a melody he would play with us as the instrument. We caricature the self-portrait he would paint. Hence all sin, whatever else it is, is sacrilege.
> - C.S. Lewis[17]

Christian prayer is empowerment, and it occurs through "participation and collaboration" with God.[18] In prayer, God gives us more of God.

What does that mean? For starters, it means we learn from God.

> God is creative (Genesis 1-2), powerful (Isaiah 40.28), wise (James 3.17), resourceful (Psalm 50.10), generous (Philippians 4.19), strategic (Proverbs 3.5-6), good (Psalm 119.68), self-sufficient (Colossians 2.2-3), and has tremendous capacity for oversight (Isaiah 41.10), leadership (Matthew 20.26), and government (Isaiah 9.7).

The list of God's attributes goes on and on well before we ever arrive at the ability to create miracles or the capacity to undo our past mistakes and make everything instantly okay. Yet those seem to be the only things we ever want from God. It's strangely rude, much like asking a successful entrepreneur to be your mentor and then demanding a loan without considering any feedback on your business plan.

The Bible declares we are saints. That word means "holy people," and though we don't feel holy, it is precisely through prayer that our outer reality becomes aligned with our inner intention.

Prayer is not meant to make us safe but to make us saints.

> To the church of God ... to those who are sanctified in Christ Jesus, called to be saints,

> with all who in every place call on the name
> of Jesus Christ our Lord.
> - 1 Corinthians 1.2, KJV

This transformation from selfhood to sainthood requires we allow our character to be re-formed.

Please re-read these key words: *transformation*, *character*, and *sainthood*.

We want God to do things for us, but God is far more interested in doing things within us. He wants to empower us so we can better cooperate with him to heal the world.

Consider how much more effective would our protests and rallies would be (to say nothing of our Facebook rants and local activism!) if our loudest voices did not discredit themselves with hateful rhetoric and worse behavior.

> Nothing else can ever cure our sick world
> except saints; and saints are never made
> except by prayer ... nothing but saints can
> save our world, because the deepest root of
> all the world's disease is sin, and saints are the
> antibodies that fight sin ... nothing but prayer
> can make saints because nothing but God can
> make saints, and we meet God in prayer.
> - Peter Kreeft[19]

But we must not be too harsh. Not on ourselves or on fellow believers. After all, not even the great heroes of our faith were perfect. John Calvin destroyed priceless works of art. John Wesley was a terrible husband to all three of his wives. Thomas Aquinas was so obese they had to cut away his seat at the dinner table. St. Francis of Assisi dumped ashes all over his food so he wouldn't be tempted to enjoy it. Julian of Norwich couldn't distinguish between an orgasm and an invocation. Origen cut off his own balls.

How much worse would they have been without prayer?

> Whatever we think about when we are free to think about whatever we will—that is what we are or will soon become.
> - A.W. Tozer[20]

And this is why we must pray: to change. Prayer makes us saints, and in the final analysis only saints can make a difference. The reason we struggle against this provocative truth is that we have forgotten that even the saints were sinners, like us. But sinners must pray, too. Not only so our sins are forgiven. Not only so we sin less in the future. But because we learn from God how to be like God. We need more of God, and so does everyone else.

Prayer does not flow from holiness, but holiness from prayer.

We pray to become like God, to become God's, and to refine ourselves into the people God designed us to be.

PROFILE

IGNATIUS OF LOYOLA
SPAIN
1491-1556

Ignatius was a man's man—a soldier, tactician, and diplomat. After being hit with a cannonball, he devoted the remainder of his life to winning spiritual battles instead of military conquests. His unique perspective gave him visions of an alternative method of spirituality. Rather than relying upon the priesthood to mediate our relationship with God, Ignatius encouraged people to examine their own lives and attend to the voice of God's Spirit within.

I admire Ignatius' commitment to trying whatever worked, including living alone in a cave, becoming a hermit, marching solo on the Holy Land, and thumbing his nose at authority (albeit temporarily).

In 1539 Ignatius, along with two friends, formed the Jesuit Order of the Catholic Church—missionaries who sought to win others to Christ through education, health care, and friendship.

> Lord, teach me to be generous.
> Teach me to serve you as you deserve;
> to give and not to count the cost,
> to fight and not to heed the wounds,

to toil and not to seek for rest,
to labor and not to ask for reward,
save that of knowing that I do your holy will.
- Prayer for Generosity[21]

Among his many contributions to Christian spirituality, Ignatius developed spiritual exercises. In brief, these rely on three forms of prayer:

Meditation: guiding our thoughts to consider the things of God.

Contemplation: more feeling than thinking, contemplation involves using our imaginations to insert ourselves into the biblical story and re-live the gospel.

Discernment: paying attention to our desires, passions, and motivations in order to ensure that they are leading us more deeply into God's presence rather than away from him

If you want to pray like Ignatius, begin by spending a few moments in each of the three phases, offering your whole heart to God.

DID YOU TEST THE EXERCISE?

Yes!

No.

WAS IT HELPFUL?

Yes!

No.

Partly...

WOULD YOU REPEAT IT?

Yes!

No.

Notes:

ACTIVE PRAYER EXERCISE

Active pray-ers may enjoy an exercise requiring a little imagination.

Set up a meeting with God. Pick a time, a location, and a duration. Prepare for the meeting as though it were any other—bring notes, a laptop, and any key information. Arrive on time and dressed for the occasion. If the meeting takes place at a coffee shop, you'll know everything you need. On the other hand, if the meeting is at a gazebo near a lake, you'll have to prepare differently.

Pray during this meeting. But don't think of it as prayer. Think of it as a meeting. Be charming and attentive. Listen. Consider what a win-win scenario might look like. Mull over the possibility of a merger. Or a relationship.

When the meeting is over, send follow-up correspondence—an email, for example, or a printed note.

These kinds of visualizations and role-play exercises get us into a healthier frame of mind for understanding that God is a person. When we imagine God in our world, we come closest to perceiving the reality behind the name Emmanuel: God with us.

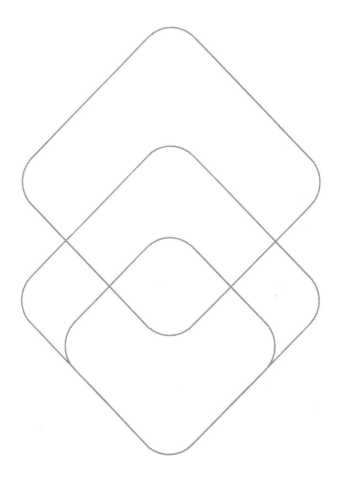

DID YOU TEST THE EXERCISE?

Yes!

No.

WAS IT HELPFUL?

Yes!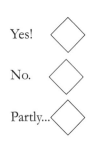

No.

Partly...

WOULD YOU REPEAT IT?

Yes!

No.

Notes:

CONTEMPLATIVE PRAYER
EXERCISE

One of Ignatius' classic spiritual practices is called The Examen, and it goes through a five-step process:

1. Become **aware** of God's presence. Ask God to show you where and how he was working over the course of your day.
2. Review the day with **gratitude**. Thank God for all that he has permitted you to enjoy.
3. Pay attention to your **emotions**. Sometimes God speaks to us through our emotions. Which of yours felt like him? Which felt like you were out of control?
4. Choose one feature of the day and **pray** from it. Highlight something important and ask God for help and guidance in the future.
5. Look toward **tomorrow**. Ask God for strength and wisdom for the following day. You know you'll need it, and it's better to fill up before you run out of gas.

THE IGNATIAN EXAMEN

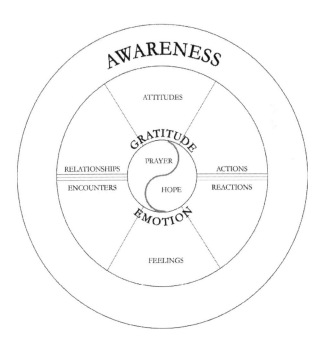

HACK

R.E.N.E.W.

Using the acronym R.E.N.E.W., ask God to help you further your spiritual journey.

- Ask God to help you **Rekindle** the flame of your spiritual passion.
- **Empty** yourself of all selfish desires.
- **Notice** what God says to you in response.
- Imagine yourself **Entering** into his presence more fully.
- Take time to experience God's presence in **Worship.**

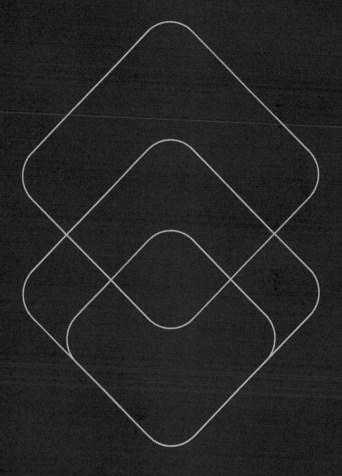

PRAYING THE SCRIPTURES

1 PETER 2

One of the most memorable sections of the Second Testament contains a reference to our new identity as a holy priesthood. Since much of Chapter Three discusses that prayer makes us saints, I thought it would be fitting to pray this piece of the Bible.

> But you are a chosen people, a royal priesthood, a holy nation, God's special possession, that you may declare the praises of him who called you out of darkness into his wonderful light. Once you were not a people, but now you are the people of God; once you had not received mercy, but now you have received mercy.
> **- 1 Peter 2.9-10, NIV**

Here's how I would pray this:

> *Thank you for choosing me, for calling me one of your own. Thank you for inviting me to be part of your royal family, an heir to a kingdom I did not build and in which I must still learn to live. Thank you for the privilege of serving as one of your priests. Please help me introduce others into your presence, and grow in my understanding of that presence daily.*

Since I belong to you, I want to celebrate. I want to tell the world that my life is better with you than it was before—brighter, warmer, more in bloom and full of life. Your Spirit gathers me. I've got new strength. I've got new hope.

Thank you for not giving up on me. Thank you for not condemning me.

Thank you.

Amen.

YOUR PRAYER:

....

....

....

....

....

....

....

DATE:

PRAYER
IS NOT
AUTOMATIC,
BUT IT
CAN BE
ORDINARY

We pray only as well as we live.
- A.W. Tozer[22]

From the beginning, our first breaths were God's.

In Eden, God created humanity out of the dust.
God breathed his Spirit into us and we came alive.
Immediately afterward, God caused trees to grow up
out of the ground. Trees, you recall, serve primarily
to produce oxygen. The Tree of Life, central to Eden,
produced the air of Paradise.

But we were cut off from Eden, cast out of the
garden and made to wander. We lost our spiritual
oxygen supply. The new air to which we had access
was something less than Eden, something … worldly.

Fortunately, our spiritual oxygen was restored
with Pentecost. In Acts 2 we're told that the Spirit
descended upon all believers. The word Spirit, *pneuma*,
means breath as much as it means animating energy.
We have been re-oxygenated, re-energized, and
revitalized with God.

All that to say, you can't measure your commitment
to God by how many hours you spend on your
knees. Prayer is like breathing—the more we pray, the
more oxygenated we become. Prayer is a continuous
conversation, and in the same way we can't go without
oxygen for more than a few minutes, we cannot persist
without prayer.

We can pray all the time, even when we're not technically praying—though that doesn't mean prayer is automatic, just that it can be ordinary. In the Christian tradition, we call this ceaseless prayer "practicing the presence of God" and, according to Leonard Sweet, it is "the key insight" into what makes prayer "Christian."

> [The name of God] YHWH, is actually uttered breath. *YH - inhale (yah) WH - exhale (weh)*. God's unutterable name can be muttered without speaking, without moving tongue or lips. Thus every person born into the world speaks the un-utterable name of God right after birth and just before they die. God is *ruach* or *pneuma*, breath or spirit, after all.
> - Len Sweet[23]

The goal is to always be with God, and—good news—we can be. The best means of reaching God is to perform mundane tasks and sacralize them—to extract the infinite from the ordinary. So, prayer can be as simple as a little thought tossed to heaven while working on heavy machinery or as complex as a long and well-constructed petition for a family member. Our hands may be at work, but our hearts and mind are with God.

I understand why this is difficult to grasp. A.W. Tozer, one of our most prolific voices on Christian prayer, claimed perceiving "our daily labors as acts of worship" was one of the most critical, yet impossible, tasks.[24] But this is what St. Paul undoubtedly meant when he said "Whatever we do, we're meant to do it for the Lord" (Colossians 3.23), and that we should "pray without ceasing" (1 Thessalonians 5.17). "Praying while working" doesn't mean we're giving God short-shrift, only halfway paying attention to him; rather, it means we're bringing God with us to work, into our homes, and into our hobbies. As C.S. Lewis said, "We can ignore, but we can nowhere evade, the presence of God."[25]

Prayer can be verbal or non-verbal; whispered, shouted, thought, or mumbled. And though not everything is prayer, anything can be. The distinction is in the orientation of our hearts. When I shout my frustration, for example, am I aiming that frustration at the Lord, trusting him to heal me of it, or shouting as an outlet for my anger?

Prayer is not so much an activity as it is a way of life. When we pray, we're making ourselves available to God. We listen to him, we attend to his nudges and nuances, and we fine-tune our awareness so we're considerate of God's desires, pleasures, and ambitions for us, through us, and with us.

Do you realize what a liberating experience this is, to know that prayer is not a chore but a posture?

> Jesus is apt to come into the very midst of life at its most real and inescapable moments. Not in a blaze of unearthly light, not in the midst of a sermon, not in the throes of some kind of religious daydream, but ... at supper

time, or walking along a road ... He never
approached from on high, but always in the
midst, in the midst of people, in the midst of
real life and the questions that real life asks.
- Frederick Buechner[26]

Despite my ardent desire to please God, I've never
wanted to pray for hours a day, trapped in a dark
room and struggling earnestly to stop being angry. I'm
convinced God wants his people to live, and prayer is
meant to draw us nearer to God and the life God both
created and intends for us to enjoy.

Do not pray about life as a means of escaping it.
Instead, take the advice of the prophet Jeremiah
and perform your normal activities in obedience to
God: "Build homes and settle down; plant gardens
and eat what they produce. Marry and have sons and
daughters ... seek the peace and prosperity of the city
into which I have carried you ..." (Jeremiah 29.5-7,
NIV).

Our prayers do not have to be fancy, or prepared in
advance, or formally scripted. I am a practitioner of
free-form prayer, which means I pray like I talk. Not
everyone is comfortable with this approach, namely
because they're wary of treating the omniscient
Creator of the Universe like a pal from the pub.
I understand this concern. And, despite the fact
that Jesus told us we were his friends (John 15.15),
that God is our Abba (Mark 14.26; Romans 8.15;
Galatians 4.6), that we are heirs with Christ to all God
commands (Romans 8.16-18), and that we are meant

to come boldly before God's throne (Hebrews 4.16),
it does seem appropriate to recognize that God is not
Gary and Christ isn't Christy from second grade.

To whit, I remember hearing Phyllis Tickle, founding
editor of the religion department at *Publisher's Weekly*,
remark that praying the liturgy was akin to "saying
words others have successfully uttered without being
killed" when approaching God. Anglican Bishop
Tom Wright picks up the same thread, referring to
our "holy boldness" when we pray, demonstrating an
"almost cheeky celebration of sheer grace."[27]

> God is the only person from whom you can
> hide nothing. Before him you will unavoidably
> come to see yourself in a new, unique light.
> Prayer, therefore, leads to a self-knowledge
> that is impossible to achieve any other way.
> - Timothy Keller[28]

The 1999 cult film *Dogma* demonstrated that
it's possible to depower Christ through over-
familiarization. In the movie, we're told that the
Roman Catholic Church has rebranded itself in an
effort to stay in step with the culture, replacing the
Suffering Servant with the Buddy Christ, shown giving
the thumbs-up.

There is danger in being cavalier with Christ, which is
why many people raise their eyebrows when we begin
our petitions with "Dear Jesus" or "Dear God," "as

though we had turned supplication into a greeting card".[29]

> To pray is to stand before God, to enter into an immediate and personal relationship with him; it is to know at every level of our being, from the instinctive to the intellectual, from the sub to the supra-conscious, that we are in God and God is in us.
> - Kallistos Ware[30]

In the end, we must think less about praying than about becoming prayers. Prayer isn't something we do; it's something we are. I liken prayer to marriage, in that marriage isn't something we perform, but a covenant into which we are wholly invested. To be married is to be in constant relationship with another person. There's never a time I'm not married to Carmel. Even if we're not together, she's on my mind. I'm conscious of what she would appreciate, or find interesting, or use. I text her throughout the day because I'm thinking about her. These communications are rarely elegant (I usually just type: *xoxo*), but they keep us tethered.

This is how we must think about our relationship with God and sustain it, also. Sometimes it is appropriate to spend hours alone with him, but that is not the only way to proceed. Neither is it the most effective way to become the people he intends. Constant communication with God will result in greater transformation than one or two sacrificial sessions on our knees.

> [The presence of God] is the habitual, silent
> and secret conversation of the soul with God.
> - Brother Lawrence[31]

I completed my doctoral research in 2005, studying the
various manifestations of spirituality on the Internet.
At the time, cyberspirituality was a novel idea that
generated no shortage of controversy. Though social
mediums like Facebook or Snapchat have brought
the communal aspect of spirituality to the fore, my
research focused on how we might pray through
the Internet. In other words, I was interested in the
direct experience of God, rather than the communal
expression of his people.

I developed an online prayer exercise called The
Prayground. It most closely resembled a video game.
The interface worked like a DJ's mixing station,
allowing users to cobble together various icons,
devotional readings, and personal reflections to be
shared online. Sadly, after only one year, the site
was hacked by pornographers and I lost my source
files; but I mention The Prayground because it
demonstrates my long-term commitment to visual and
kinesthetic prayer.

Again, we pray who we are. If we are artists, we
pray artistically. We can pray while sculpting, while
doodling, while creating objects both trivial and
transcendent. And we don't only pray *while* we're doing
these things, but also *through* them. Our art becomes
a prayer in and of itself, so long as we consciously
wrestle our hearts toward him. If we are athletes,

our training or performance may be prayer. If we
are business people, our cooperative ventures or
entrepreneurial engagements may be prayer. Because
whenever we are consecrated to God, all our works are
offered up to him, also.

But we must be careful whenever we create something
of our prayer. When we paint our prayer, for example,
there is great temptation for us to admire that painting,
maybe even to sell it. We might wonder if a book on
prayer isn't especially lucid, and if such writings might
not be the manner of our ascent to public life. This is
perilous territory, for once we decide to commodify
our prayer, we begin to perform for the camera—like
reality television in which we must falsify tension to
hold audience interest.

Do not let your ego profit from prayer.

> When I left the King, I began to rehearse
> what I would say to the world: long rehearsals
> full of revisions, imaginary applause,
> humiliations, edicts of revenge. I grew swollen
> as I conspired with my ambition, I struggled,
> I expanded, and when the term was up, I gave
> birth to an ape. After some small inevitable
> misunderstanding, the ape turned on me.
> Limping, stumbling, I fled back to the swept
> courtyards of the King. 'Where is your ape?'
> the King demanded. 'Bring me your ape.'
> The work is slow. The ape is old. He clowns
> behind his bars, imitating our hands in the
> dream. He winks at my official sense of

urgency. What King, he wants to know. What
courtyard? What highway?
- Leonard Cohen[32]

We are all beginners, and my aim is to help beginners
realize that prayer is easier and more ordinary than we
might assume.

We can practice God's presence regardless of what is
happening around us. God is with us, regardless of
where we are. God is in us, regardless of the mess
we're in. God moves through us, regardless of our
movements.

And the more we become attuned to God, the more
God teaches us to stay in tune with his plans to heal
the world.

PROFILE

BROTHER LAWRENCE
FRANCE
1614-1691

There is no brighter light than Brother Lawrence, whose famous book *The Practice of the Presence of God* has liberated prayer from religion for millions of Christians.

By all accounts, Brother Lawrence was a woefully unsuccessful monk, easily caricaturized as a buffoon shambling around the monastery and causing his friars a never-ending series of frustrations, furies, and face-palms. He worked in the kitchens, mostly, and spent his later years repairing shoes, though there are whispers he was finally tasked with keeping bees. With no historical evidence to support this, I nevertheless like to imagine the friar gave him this job out of spite, and that Lawrence often had honey on his chin.

Lawrence developed a method of prayer wherein he attuned his mind and heart to God at all times. Rather than formal prayers, he disciplined himself to "practice the presence" of God. This wasn't automatic, but it became his ordinary way of life.

> [God] does not ask much of us, merely a
> thought of Him from time to time, a little act

of adoration, sometimes to ask for His grace, sometimes to offer Him your sufferings, at other times to thank Him for the graces, past and present, He has bestowed on you, in the midst of your troubles, to take solace in Him as often as you can. Lift up your heart to Him during your meals and in company; the least little remembrance will always be the most pleasing to Him. One need not cry out very loudly; He is nearer to us than we think.
- Brother Lawrence[33]

If you want to pray like Brother Lawrence, here's how you might begin:

1. Start and complete each day by **inviting the Spirit** to govern your thoughts and behaviors.
2. Choose something simple that will **serve as a prompt** throughout the day—the hourly beep of your watch or a figurine on your desk. When prompted, pray and once again turn your thoughts to God, inviting him to speak to you.
3. Regularly take time to jot down little **notes and observations** about what God may be saying to you, and review those when you return home at the end of the day.

The goal is a continuous awareness of God. These steps are easy ways to begin, but I'm sure you get the idea that the steps themselves have no power. Feel free to adapt them or discard them, so long as you find good ways to attune yourself to the Spirit.

ACTIVE PRAYER EXERCISE

DID YOU TEST THE EXERCISE?

Yes!

No.

WAS IT HELPFUL?

Yes!

No.

Partly...

WOULD YOU REPEAT IT?

Yes!

No.

Notes:

My friend Ken Brewer[34] taught me one of the simplest exercises, and yet one of the most meaningful. Instead of setting aside a specific time of day for prayer, pray every time you walk. When you walk from your car to your office, pray. When you walk across campus, pray. When you walk the dog, pray. By consecrating your walking time, you'll train yourself to be mindful of God's presence more frequently, thereby giving you a much easier time of turning your thoughts toward him.

And, if you hardly walk and would prefer to try something else, this exercise works equally well with "driving time" or "outdoor time." Likewise, if you're musical, you may replace praying with singing, since any distinction between prayer and praise is trivial at best.

Enjoy!

CONTEMPLATIVE PRAYER
EXERCISE

DID YOU TEST THE EXERCISE?

Yes!

No.

WAS IT HELPFUL?

Yes!

No.

Partly...

WOULD YOU REPEAT IT?

Yes!

No.

Notes:

The Jesus Prayer is a short, simple prayer that is often repeated many times in a single session. In fact, many in the Eastern Orthodox Church will set a goal of praying this prayer 1,500-3,000 times in a day, since the purpose of the repetition is to allow us to lose focus on the words and experience, instead, a kind of mystical union with God.

The common term for prayers like this is mantra, though many in the Christian tradition are uncomfortable with it since it feels so foreign. But words are just signifiers, and in any case, we never need to be wary of praying to Christ.

If you're a fan of *Star Wars*, you may recall the character of Chirrut Inwe in *Rogue One*, who repeated a similar mantra in tense situations, proclaiming: *I am one with the Force and the Force is with me.*

Here is the Jesus Prayer:

> *Lord Jesus,*
> *Son of God,*
> *Have mercy on me,*
> *A sinner.*

HACK

THE TRICLINIUM MEDITATION

My understanding of prayer changed dramatically once I learned about tricliniums.

Triclinium comes from two Greek words meaning "three" (*tri*) "couches" (*kline*), and it refers both to the furniture and the room in which that furniture was placed—the formal dining room in a traditional Roman home. Three chaise lounges were pushed together in an overlapping zig-zag, thereby creating a space in the middle for servants, entertainers, and teachers. Each couch would have been big enough for a family to share, though it was common for three adults to lie together, also.

TRICLINIUM MEDITATION

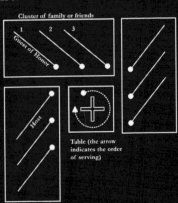

Positions of guests reclining in a triclinium

In Matthew 18, Jesus tells his followers that "wherever two or three are gathered in [his] name, [he] is in their midst." The phrase "in the midst" refers to the center of a triclinium.

Once I realized this, my paradigm for prayer shifted. Prayer became more social, more pleasant, and more interesting. Since "the midst" of the triclinium had specific functions, it was marvelous to consider that Christ was placing himself in the role of a servant. Of course he did this many times, but it's strange to think he's doing it once again. It's humbling.

Likewise, Christ in the midst comes to entertain—to sing and perform. So prayer doesn't have to be dour or miserable. Jesus wants us to lighten up, to liven up, and to enjoy what he's offering.

Finally, Christ-in-the-midst comes to educate; which, in the ancient world, was always meant to be a conversation. He wants to teach, but his instruction requires we ask questions, debate, and sometimes arrive at our own conclusions.

I want you to pray imagining Christ in your midst. Ask these questions to guide you:

- How is Christ welcoming you into his presence? Welcome him in return.
- What is Christ serving to nourish and sustain you? Thank him for it.
- What joys has Christ prepared? Appreciate them, and him, for these blessings.
- What is Christ teaching you? Submit to his authority.

PRAYING THE SCRIPTURES

PSALM 121

Psalm 121 is one of the Psalms of Ascent, sung on
pilgrimage to Jerusalem. That means these were prayed
while walking, and since walking prayer is one of the
recommended exercises for this chapter, I thought
we'd explore the psalm and how to pray it.

> I lift up my eyes to the mountains—
>   where does my help come from?
> My help comes from the Lord,
>   the Maker of heaven and earth.
> The Lord watches over you—
>   the Lord is your shade at your right hand;
> the sun will not harm you by day,
>   nor the moon by night.
> The Lord will keep you from all harm—
>   he will watch over your life;
> the Lord will watch over your coming and
> going
>   both now and forevermore.
> **Psalm 121, NIV**

Here's how I would pray this:

> *God, I'm looking to you for help because I've got
> nowhere else to go. I refuse to wallow. I look to you,
> instead, trusting that you can sustain me. You are the
> Great God of the heavens, Maker and Sustainer of
> worlds; I figure, if you can do all that, you can help
> me.*

Teach me to walk with confidence and holiness. Teach help me to sleep soundly and find short times for rest during the day. Show me how to manage my time and my energy so I can be strong for my children and good to Carmel. Don't let me overcommit or make foolish decisions about my time, and please protect me from the hyper-sensitivity that permeates our world. I want to be useful, productive, healthy, and happy. I think you want that, too.

Teach me to be mindful of you at all times and in all places, listening to your voice and paying attention to your nudges. I don't ever want to ignore you or shut you out. Everywhere I am, you are, and I want to appreciate that connection more fully.

Amen.

YOUR PRAYER:

DATE:

THE
MOST
COMMON
CAUSE
OF
UNANSWERED
PRAYER

*Perhaps the best metaphor to describe our hurried
and distracted lives is that of a car wash. When you
pull up to a car wash, you are instructed to leave your
motor running, to take your hands off the steering
wheel, and to keep your foot off the brake. The idea
is that the machine itself will suck you through ...
for most of us, that's just what our typical day does to
us—it sucks us through.*
- Ronald Rolheiser[35]

I've been counseling couples for almost twenty
years. During that time, I've had more than a few
conversations with frustrated women. One especially
sticks out in my mind, where an attractive, well-put-
together young lady set a tearful appointment for
advice.

"He just doesn't communicate," she began.

I knew she was talking about her betrothed.
He was often a disappointment. "At all?"

"He whispers," she scoffed. "But how am I
supposed to listen for a whisper in the middle
of kids and chores and work and school? It's
asinine."

"He never says anything plainly?"

"Oh sure—lots of things," she allowed. "But
there's so many it's difficult to figure out what
he really wants."

I nodded, beginning to put the picture together in my mind. "Do you find it hard to get a word in edgewise?"

She shook her head. "He loves to write letters, but I don't want to have to read in order to talk, you know? I just wish he was more ... normal."

Her anger surprised me. In my experience, most women would be very grateful for that level of intimacy.

I decided on another tact. "What do his friends say?" I asked.

She rolled her eyes. "They're convinced he's perfect. But I'm like—hey—I'm not the problem here. He's not even human."

If we are the bride of Christ, it sometimes feels as though we need couple's counseling. It's hard to get anything out of him—he won't share his feelings, he won't lift a finger around his house, and he's hard to read.

But if we did go to counseling with Christ, I suspect most of us would know what we're really up to: we're trying to change him, rather than taking a hard look at ourselves.

That's the problem with marriage counseling, and also with prayer. We think the other person is at fault, and that we're there just to be supportive while they work out their issues. But if there's one altruism that holds in both scenarios it's this: *you can't change him.*

The number one problem in most relationships is communication, and there's a breakdown between us and God. But the problem isn't God. It's us. If anything, God has over-communicated—he speaks to us through his Word, his Church, and his Spirit. But we don't read his Word enough to know what he says or thinks or feels. And we tend to disregard his Church. And it's hard to listen to the still small voice of his Spirit over the cacophony of cultural distraction.

I understand why this is hard. After all, sometimes prayer feels like conversation with an invalid. It's like we got engaged to someone we think is perfect, but something happens and they slip into a coma. They're in the hospital, and we love them, so we visit. We wipe their chin and speak tenderly as they sip their milk. Maybe they look at us when we squeeze their hand. We leave. We feel okay. But it's tough to want to come back.

We feel like we're the ones doing everything. God is a disappointment.

But we're not playing fair, are we? We haven't exercised that which our counselor recommends. We haven't been to physical therapy with our invalid. We've just looked at God—either across the room or on the couch—and thought: *he should be better.*

We need to stop trying to fix God and begin to listen to what God is saying. He's speaking all the time, and the reason we can't hear him is because we're inattentive. Like a busy fiancée, we can't be bothered. Like a hospital visitor, we're too busy feeling sorry for ourselves to realize God is clear-eyed and smiling, eager for conversation.

> What most of all hinders heavenly
> consolation is that you are too slow in turning
> yourself to prayer.
> - Thomas à Kempis[36]

Much of our disappointment concerns unanswered prayer. But the most common cause of unanswered prayer is prayerlessness.[37] Consider the last time you brought something to God in prayer. Did you passionately pray about it, or have you only mentioned it? Have you only liked the Facebook page most closely associated with the issue? Have you wallowed in God's failure to answer a prayer you've never bothered to articulate?

As famed pastor Bill Hybels has painstakingly pointed out, most of us cannot be trusted to lift up our requests to God "fervently and regularly over an extended period of time."[38]

And, with only two exceptions, he's right.

You already know the exceptions, don't you? Healing for the terminally ill and romance for the perpetually single. I don't mean to make light of either, since they both demonstrate a solid understanding that our deepest wounds belong in the safest place—with God. But, setting those aside momentarily, it is rare for us to pray with any perseverance, persistence, or pattern.

For example, people often request prayer for help with their finances. I am happy to oblige, but always feel compelled to follow up. I ask them if they've been praying about the issue. The answer is always yes. But when I ask how many hours over the last eight days they've prayed, there is stunned silence. I do this deliberately, since I've learned that people will fudge how many minutes they've prayed but rarely have the foresight to manufacture a set number of hours. It's okay. I don't want them to feel guilty. I just want to expose the fact that, so far, this isn't really something they're taking to God.

And they should.

When we're in financial trouble we ought to be asking God for opportunities to generate revenue, to find work, to develop our skills, to manage our money, to be generous in the midst of our poverty, to trust more, to need less, and to maintain a sweet Spirit. I know this because I have been poor and have prayed about it intensely for many, many hours. There's only so many times you can say, "God please help me get some money so we can make it" before God starts speaking back. And when God responds, he rarely says "Ok— got it. Go have fun!"

As much as prayer is practicing the presence of God, it also involves seasons of sustained petition wherein we bring our requests to God (Philippians 4.6), trusting that God will help (John 14.13) if we're persistent (Matthew 7.7).

When I'm in need of real help on a particular issue, I find it useful to imagine that God is deep inside me and my prayers are little shovels slowly excavating my soul. No matter how much or how intensely I pray, it's going to take some time to get all the way to the bottom. But I know it'll be worth it, so I keep digging. The closer I get to God, the more his heat and energy and light start to leak through the heartsoil. Eventually, I break open the cavern and he's brilliant—I've struck gold.

But it takes time.

If we want God involved in our lives, we'll need to invest. We'll need to talk. We'll need to listen. That can sometimes feel frustrating, but, as Mother Teresa was fond of saying "God does not demand that we are successful. God demands that we are faithful."

Faithfulness requires patience; and patience, strength.

These are given when we pray.

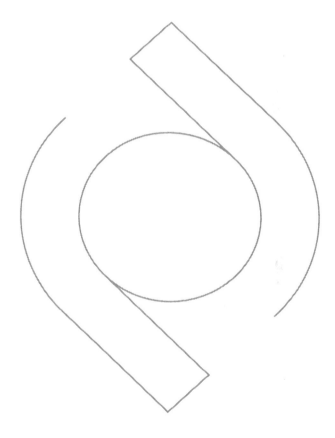

PROFILE ATHANASIUS OF ALEXANDRIA EGYPT, 296-373

God became man that we might become
gods.
- Athanasius[39]

Athanasius was a firebrand who spent most of his
life in exile because he couldn't keep his mouth shut.
He was so passionate for the truth, and so persistent
in proclaiming the Trinitarian nature of God, that he
refused to let sloppy thinking and doctrinal error go
unchallenged. He was an agitator, an irritant, and an
antagonist. This earned him the moniker "Athanasius
Against Everyone."

Nevertheless, he was well regarded by his orthodox
peers and soon came to be known as the first "Pillar
of the Church." Likewise, he was one of the earliest
people to articulate Christian spirituality as *theosis*—the
union of the human and the divine. Jesus, of course,
meant for us to understand it in these terms when
he said, "whoever lives in God, lives in me." Because
we're not imitating Christ, but incarnating Christ.
Christ isn't out there, but inside each of us, animating
us and metamorphosing us into new creations.

For God is good - or rather, of all goodness
He is the Fountainhead.
- Athanasius[40]

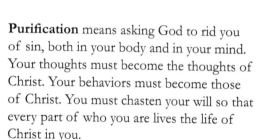

If you want to pray like Athanasius, you'll need
to consider two crucial details: purification and
illumination.

Purification means asking God to rid you
of sin, both in your body and in your mind.
Your thoughts must become the thoughts of
Christ. Your behaviors must become those
of Christ. You must chasten your will so that
every part of who you are lives the life of
Christ in you.

Illumination means pursuing God with such
fervor that he reveals himself in moments
of profound mental and spiritual clarity.
Sometimes this may involve visions or dreams,
and sometimes this may simply be strong
feelings or impressions; regardless, please
understand that it is only the very devoted
who experience this kind of union with their
Maker.

To begin, I suggest starting with 10 minutes of prayer
asking God to purify you (and to heighten your
sensitivity to future sin), followed by 10 minutes of
prayer asking God to reveal himself more fully to you.

ACTIVE PRAYER
EXERCISE

DID YOU TEST THE EXERCISE?

Yes!

No.

WAS IT HELPFUL?

Yes!

No.

Partly...

WOULD YOU REPEAT IT?

Yes!

No.

Notes:

Active pray-ers need something to do, and often the simplest solutions are best. I recommend keeping a prayer journal—either on paper or on your phone. If you use paper, take time each day to write down your requests, leaving space for you to note if and when God answers them. If you're like most people, you'll be surprised at how often God does *actually* answer prayer.

If you're not a writer, consider leaving yourself voicemails or using the speech-to-text function on your phone to keep track of your prayers. For what it's worth, this is my favorite way to pray. I pray while speaking into my phone, and then I pray while playing the recording back to me. I delete the prayer once it's been answered, or amend it, thereby keeping a constant log of my time with God.

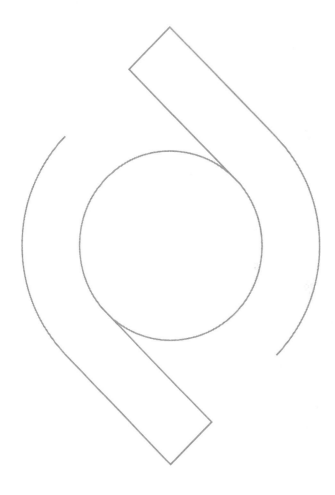

**DID YOU
TEST THE
EXERCISE?**

Yes!

No.

**WAS IT
HELPFUL?**

Yes!

No.

Partly...

**WOULD YOU
REPEAT IT?**

Yes!

No.

Notes:

CONTEMPLATIVE PRAYER
EXERCISE

There has been no more helpful prayer tool for me than spiritual breathing. It's a simple exercise, wherein you govern your thoughts according to the rhythms of your breath. When you exhale, you pray for God to remove sinful "carbon dioxides" (like lust, rage, victimization, etc.). When you inhale, you pray for God to oxygenate you with his Spirit (filling you with love, joy, peace, etc.). I also find it helpful to say "Yahweh" as I inhale (*Yaw-*) and exhale (*-weh*), since it is an easy method of visualizing God's Spirit working through me.

> [We] need the divine breath...The name of God disclosed to Moses, ehyeh asher ehyeh, with "h" and "sh" sounds, "is as near as we can get in language to pure breath," according to British novelist Gabriel Josipovici, one of the leading literary theorists in the world today.
> - Leonard Sweet[41]

This is an easy exercise to master, but mastery never reduces the benefits. Every day, I take between twelve to fifteen moments where I practice spiritual breathing. It helps calm my anxiety, reduce my irritation, and gives me much-needed empathy in difficult circumstances.

SPIRITUAL BREATHING

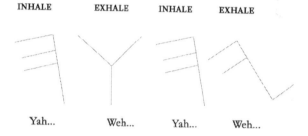

INHALE   EXHALE   INHALE   EXHALE

Yah...   Weh...   Yah...   Weh...

HACK

WRITTEN PRAYER

Writing down your prayers is a simple means of keeping focused. This is especially helpful if you struggle with your thoughts racing around like untrained apes.

Writing is the most important part, since it affects memory retention and comprehension so heavily. Don't worry if you write your prayers on loose-leaf papers or Post-it® notes. You can collect those later, or just keep everything in a scrapbook. It doesn't matter. The point is to constrain your thoughts to words.

Every day, write down the following things:

- 3 things for which you're thankful.
- 3 people who need help and how.
- 3 ways you hope God can help you change
- Anything else you think God might be saying to you.

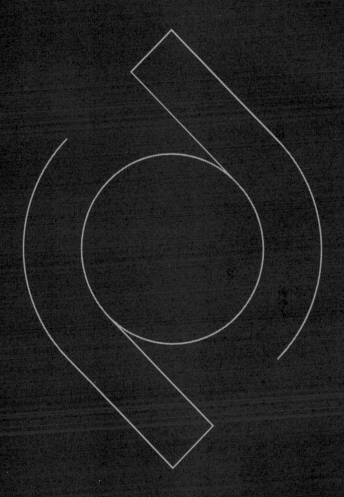

PRAYING THE SCRIPTURES

EPHESIANS 3

St. Paul's letter to the church in Ephesus focuses on what it means to live as God's people, constantly connected to him. Since that connection is a significant theme in this chapter, I thought a prayer from Ephesians was appropriate.

> I pray that out of his glorious riches God may strengthen you with power through his Spirit in your inner being, so that Christ may dwell in your hearts through faith. And I pray that you, being rooted and established in love, may have power, together with all the Lord's holy people, to grasp how wide and long and high and deep is the love of Christ, and to know this love that surpasses knowledge—that you may be filled to the measure of all the fullness of God.
>
> **Ephesians 3.16-19, NIV**

Here's how I would pray this:

> *God—I know that you have energy to spare and are willing to loan it out, and that you've got resources I can't possibly understand. So I'm asking you to help. Help me become strong. Help me become wise. Fill me with more of your grace and peace and truth. Teach me how to love more wholly and more joyously. I want to draw more deeply on your love when I feel weak.*

Teach me the true meaning of power, and how to use what little power I have to bless and heal your people. Everything I have comes from you, through you, and is meant to be used for your glory. Please help me to be faithful with it. Please fill me up in excess of my understanding, so I can work with you to heal the world.

Amen.

YOUR PRAYER:

....

....

....

....

....

....

....

....

DATE:

WHY PRAYER DOESN'T WORK

The New Testament contains embarrassing promises that what we pray for with faith we shall receive. Mark 11.24 is the most staggering. "Whatever we ask for, believing that we'll get it." No question, it seems, of confining it to "spiritual" things, "whatever we ask for." No question of a merely general faith in God, but a belief that you will get the particular thing you ask. No question of getting either it or else something that is really far better for you; you'll get precisely it.
- *C.S. Lewis[42]*

Now we get to the big question: *Why doesn't prayer work?*

Why don't we get what we want when we pray? In the previous chapter, we talked about the fact that the chief cause of unanswered prayer is prayerlessness. But what about those times when we do pray—passionately, faithfully, for hours? For years?

And what about those issues when the outcomes are clearly good and well within the bounds of God's will according to Scripture—like healing for the sick, or clarity about a difficult situation, or relief from adverse circumstances? In times like these, when we're sure we're doing everything we can and we're sure what we want is right, we're left wondering: *What am I doing wrong?* And, more often, *what is wrong with God?*

I have been answering these questions almost daily for decades, but you won't like my answers, especially if you're in the middle of a painful and confusing bout with God. In fact, once I'm done, you may wonder, *what's the point of praying at all?*

Because prayer isn't about making things happen or causing change in the world. Praying isn't a means of bending God's will to ours; nor, as Tozer said, is it an "assault upon the reluctance of God."[43]

Prayer isn't about getting what we want.

If our requests are ungodly, God will not accede. If we want something good but the timing is wrong, God may caution us to slow down. If there's something rotten in us, God will often lead us along paths of character development rather than simply tossing us treats. And yet, if the timing is right and the request is godly and we are healthy, God may still sometimes decline to fulfill our requests.

Why?

Most people will tell you prayer is about intimacy with God, but I hate that word. It's exclusively feminine, and so over-used, that I feel like someone's aunt whenever I say it. Or, worse, I hear Mike Myers' character, the Love Guru, telling me that you're "into me, I see." I prefer Peter Kreeft's far more biblical assertion that the purpose of prayer is to make us saints, since "only God can make saints and we meet God in prayer,"[44] that the world needs saints if it will ever be healed, and that we must become saints if we are ever to overcome the challenges and difficulties of ordinary life.

Prayer isn't about getting what we want from God. Prayer is how we become like God by being with God. It's about learning to trust God and deepen our experience of him.

> People feel a problem about prayer because they are in a muddle about God. If you are uncertain whether God exists, or whether he is personal, or good, or in control of things, or concerned about ordinary folk like you and me, you are bound to conclude that praying is pretty pointless, not to say trivial, and then you won't do it.
> - JI Packer[45]

That's why we spoke earlier of God as our mentor, and that prayer is primarily a means of empowerment. When we spend time with God, he rubs off on us. He's wise, so we become wiser. Life is complex, confusing, and full of moral ambiguities. We need wisdom, and when we pray, we get it. Consequently, we're better equipped to handle life. God is imaginative, as are his saints. When we pray, our creative capacities increase, and we are able to solve problems, innovate, and participate in artistic endeavors more energetically as a result of time spent with our mentor.

If we have been changed for the better by our teachers, our coaches, good parents, and loving sages, how much more have we been changed by God?

Some agree that Kierkegaard said it best when he proclaimed that "The function of prayer is not to influence God, but rather to change the nature of the one who prays."[46] I'm tempted to agree, except for all the crazy stuff I've experienced that defies the defeatist logic at the heart of this statement.

On more than a dozen occasions in a variety of locations, circumstances, and across a wide spectrum of fellow participants, I've prayed and witnessed miracles. Genuine, honest-to-God miracles. The sick got well. The lame stood up and made tea. The cancer went away. The child recovered. The desire for alcohol vanished. The marriage restored overnight. Someone who was meant to die did not.

And the fact that these things happened makes it all the more frustrating that none of the other things I've prayed for have.

Because sometimes prayer works.

Why didn't God heal the person you loved? I don't know. He does sometimes, but rarely. The truth is that we all die, so any healing is only temporary. Jesus raised Lazarus from the dead, but Lazarus died a second time about thirty years later. Since we're promised new bodies in a new creation which will never age, weaken, sicken or expire, any prolonged longevity on this side of the river isn't for the benefit of the person who was healed, but for us. That doesn't mean our requests are ungodly, just that the outcomes are inevitable.

Of course you may be praying for healing so the person you love can live comfortably, rather than be spared from death. Why doesn't God more frequently answer these prayers? I don't know. Sometimes he does. I can speculate that our momentary sufferings prepare us for the eternal weight of glory (2 Corinthians 4.17), or that God is forming us into remarkable people through remarkable trials, or that his ways are not our ways (Isaiah 55.8-9), but I realize those answers don't wash when you're in the middle of the suck.

What about the people we love who suffer from mental illness, or chronic depression, or addiction? Why can't God heal them? Why doesn't he? I don't know. Sometimes he does, but here it's of critical importance to acknowledge that God will not change other people.

Full stop.

If you're praying for God to change your husband, your boss, your daughter or your friend it absolutely will not happen. Read that again. It will not happen. We cannot compel God to compel others that they might conform to our demands. You might think you're praying for God to heal them, and maybe something inside them does need to be healed, but the moment we transition away from physical ailments to anything associated with character, personality, or relationships on any level we must acknowledge that our desires are misplaced.

> [God] you are the slim crescent of a moon
> that I see and my self is the earth's shadow
> that keeps me from seeing the moon …
> What I am afraid of, dear God, is that my self
> shadow will grow so large that it blocks the
> whole moon, and that I will judge myself by
> the shadow that is nothing . I do not know
> you God because I am in the way.
> - Flannery O'Connor[47]

I realize that, so far, all I've addressed is why prayer doesn't work, when what we really want to know is how we can guarantee that it will. But there are few guarantees in prayer.

Prayer is like forgetting your password, maddeningly trying to get access to the things you know are yours. Persistent, unanswered prayer feels like you've unsuccessfully entered your password so many times you get locked out of your account entirely.

We're drawn to prayer because we think prayer has power, or that "God's power flows primarily to people that pray."[48] But the worst feeling possible isn't that God refuses us, but that he ignores us.

We're convinced that prayer is like buried treasure. If we find the "secret path" to God, we think all our problems will be solved. But what if God isn't hiding? And what if, in the middle of that hidden location, there's no treasure except himself?

We think prayer is like a seed, and if we do the miserable work of planting and watering it, eventually our duty will pay off with the best possible fruit. But what if God wants to plant and water with us, and the tree never produces anything edible? What if the tree is simply beautiful to look at, and God stands beside us in admiration?

What if we never get what we want, but what we receive instead is far better? Only, since we're angry about not getting what we want, we fail to appreciate what we've been given?

So what's the use of prayer if it isn't about getting help from God? We do get help from God, just not always in the manner of our choosing. Don't stop asking for fear that God doesn't hear or that he's reluctant to help. After all, he's the one who instructs us to ask in the first place. When we ask, we're demonstrating obedience. So pray and keep on praying, ask and keep on asking, knock and the door will be opened to you (Matthew 7.7). But don't be surprised when you come inside and the home is altogether different than you imagined.

THOMAS MERTON UNITED STATES OF AMERICA, 1915-1968

For most of my adult life I've struggled to find Christian people like me. I don't know that I'm especially different than everyone else, but the celebrities of modern Christian expression are typically too boring or too sparkly for my tastes. When they pray or sing or preach, I either struggle to stay awake or feel compelled to uncomfortably cross my legs.

But that all changed when I was introduced to Thomas Merton: activist, poet, and rogue.

Merton wrote 65 books, was a friend to both Martin Luther King Jr. and the Dalai Lama, and has been lauded by Pope Francis as one of the greatest Americans of all time. He began as a drunk and a womanizer, then found God and a healed appreciation for women and wine. He was strong, warm, and his commitment to Christ never diminished his charm, but deepened it.

Here is the most important prayer I've ever read. It's on my fridge. On my desk. In my car. And the first line is the most oft-repeated sentence in my time alone with God.

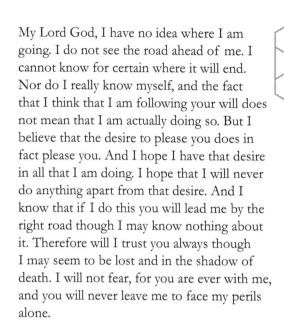

My Lord God, I have no idea where I am
going. I do not see the road ahead of me. I
cannot know for certain where it will end.
Nor do I really know myself, and the fact
that I think that I am following your will does
not mean that I am actually doing so. But I
believe that the desire to please you does in
fact please you. And I hope I have that desire
in all that I am doing. I hope that I will never
do anything apart from that desire. And I
know that if I do this you will lead me by the
right road though I may know nothing about
it. Therefore will I trust you always though
I may seem to be lost and in the shadow of
death. I will not fear, for you are ever with me,
and you will never leave me to face my perils
alone.
- Thomas Merton[49]

How can we pray like Thomas Merton? That's
like asking how to write like Ernest Hemingway.
Nevertheless, here are a few rough guidelines:

> First, **drop all pretense**. Don't try and sound
> spiritual. Just puke your guts out and trust
> God to mop away the sickness.

> Second, **forget any gimmicks**. No tricks.
> No persuasive techniques. Give up entirely on
> what you want and ask God to want what he
> wants instead. Good luck with that.

Third, go hard in two opposite directions at once: **silence and action**. Learn to sit comfortably with God. Don't fill the silence with yammering. Don't ruin the moment. Let God be your soaking tub. Then get out of the tub and get to work. Seriously. Contemplation is useless unless it translates to action.

Finally, submit yourself to the full misery of your misdeeds. Grace is free but it ain't cheap, and when you need it, you're not doing yourself any favors by pretending you don't. **Face up to your sin**. Own it. It's bad, and so are you. Then give that sin back to God and pray for his mercy. Just because he's willing to forgive doesn't mean we shouldn't be eager to beg.

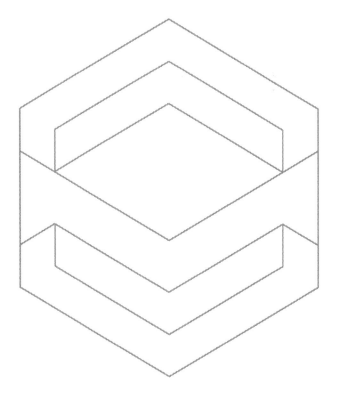

DID YOU TEST THE EXERCISE?

Yes!

No.

WAS IT HELPFUL?

Yes!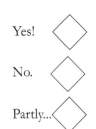

No.

Partly...

WOULD YOU REPEAT IT?

Yes!

No.

Notes:

ACTIVE PRAYER EXERCISE

I find it helpful to play with different images while praying. For active pray-ers, cycling through these metaphors will create a template for prayer and also a sense of progression. Pray to God using a different image each day:

- *Lord* (Jeremiah 32.27: "I am the Lord, the God of all flesh ...")
- *Priest* (Hebrews 4.14: "We have a high priest who has ascended into heaven, Jesus, the Son of God ...")
- *Friend* (John 15.15: "No longer do I call you servants, but friends ...")
- *Mother* (Isaiah 66.13: "As a mother comforts her young, so I will comfort you ...")
- *Creator* (Job 38.4: "Where were you when I created the foundations of the earth?")
- *Lady Wisdom* (Proverb 8.1: "Does not wisdom call out?")
- *Counselor* (Isaiah 9.6: "He shall be called Wonderful Counselor, Mighty God, Prince of Peace ...")
- *Model* (1 Peter 2.21: "Christ suffered for you, leaving you a model so you might follow in his footsteps ...")

When you pray, address God by the various titles. Imagine you're visiting with God according to the constraints of those images, and then keep a record of how this affects your conversation. For example, addressing God as your Lord might require that you kneel or show additional respect, as you imagine yourself in God's heavenly court room. Conversely, addressing God as your Counselor may require you sit on a sofa as you imagine yourself in God's home office receiving therapy.

PERSONIFICATIONS FOR PRAYER

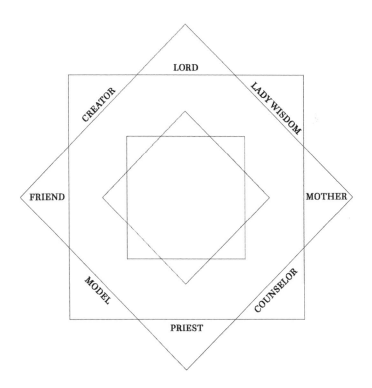

DID YOU TEST THE EXERCISE?

Yes!

No.

WAS IT HELPFUL?

Yes!

No.

Partly...

WOULD YOU REPEAT IT?

Yes!

No.

Notes:

CONTEMPLATIVE PRAYER
EXERCISE

Many contemplatives find it useful to employ icons during prayer. If you've never tried this, please don't be alarmed. An icon is an image that we use to help focus our thoughts on God. During the Reformation, many Protestants eschewed this practice because they confused it with idolatry. Consequently, thousands of icons were defaced, defamed, and destroyed. But icons are just tools. They are not substitutes for God and we need have no misgivings about their use.

If you can't find an icon, I suggest finding images on your phone from the vast collection of sacred arts available on the Internet. Find an artistic representation of God that shows God as any of the following manifestations, then pray as though God were only that and catalogue your differing experiences.

- *Lord* (Jeremiah 32.27: "I am the Lord, the God of all flesh ...")
- *Priest* (Hebrews 4.14: "We have a high priest who has ascended into heaven, Jesus, the Son of God ...")
- *Friend* (John 15.15: "No longer do I call you servants, but friends ...")
- *Mother* (Isaiah 66.13: "As a mother comforts her young, so I will comfort

you …")

- *Creator* (Job 38.4: "Where were you when I created the foundations of the earth?")
- *Lady Wisdom* (Proverbs 8.1: "Does not wisdom call out?")
- *Counselor* (Isaiah 9.6: "He shall be called Wonderful Counselor, Mighty God, Prince of Peace …")
- *Model* (1 Peter 2.21: "Christ suffered for you, leaving you a model so you might follow in his footsteps …")

PERSONIFICATIONS FOR PRAYER

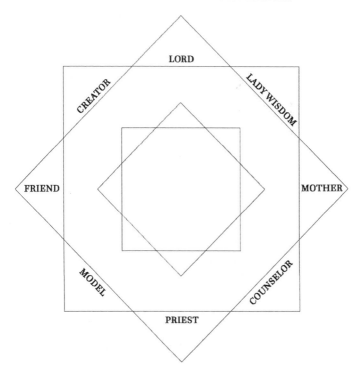

HACK

GUIDED MEDITATION

After reading this chapter, you may be feeling disappointed. Or angry. Or confused. That's okay. Take time to work through this guided meditation. Meditation is simply a way of governing our minds and is commonly considered prayer. Follow each step, exhausting your thoughts, before moving onto the next one. If you stall, count to three, then try again. If you're still stuck, return to the previous item and take a running start.

Good luck!

- Tell God what you think of him.
- Tell God the best moment from yesterday
- Acknowledge how God was involved in that moment.
- Thank God for his involvement.
- Thank God for two other times like that moment, whether in recent memory or even further back.
- Ask God for help in one area of your life.
- Ask God to reveal who you can emulate in that area, so you can model yourself after them.
- Thank God you have people you can emulate.
- Ask God to reveal the people who might be looking to you as a model.
- Ask the Lord to help you as you endeavor to help them.
- Ask God to keep you humble as you do so.
- Thank God for the privilege of shadowing Him.

HOW TO BE WITH GOD

PRAYING THE SCRIPTURES

JOHN 15

We've often discussed that prayer is how God makes
us godly, transforming us into saints. Let us now
pray through one of the key biblical passages that
demonstrates the true nature of our union with Christ.

> I am the vine; you are the branches. If you
> remain in me and I in you, you will bear much
> fruit; apart from me you can do nothing.
> If you do not remain in me, you are like
> a branch that is thrown away and withers;
> such branches are picked up, thrown into the
> fire and burned. If you remain in me and
> my words remain in you, ask whatever you
> wish, and it will be done for you. This is to
> my Father's glory, that you bear much fruit,
> showing yourselves to be my disciples.
> **John 15.5-8, NIV**

Here's how I would pray this:

> *Lord, I am nothing without you. I have no life, no
> energy, no growth, and no promise apart from you.
> I want to remind myself of this every day—that I
> am not the vine. You are. You are my source. You
> are everything I need, and you give me more than I
> require. Help me remain in you. Help me be content
> with my branch-li-ness. I do not want to be cut off
> or cast away! I want to find more joy in more of you,*

strengthening the connection as I feed on your words. I want to bear good fruit. Insofar as my desires produce that fruit, please help me with them. But if my desires are weird or misplaced, or they look good but are actually bad on the inside, please forgive me. Please interrupt me. Because I want to glorify you with even my secret thoughts.

Amen.

YOUR PRAYER:

DATE:

STRANGE
AND
UNCOMFORTABLE

> *We pray less for God than for one another. He doesn't*
> *benefit from the recognition. We benefit from the*
> *reminder.*
> *- The Church Survival Guide[50]*

There is a distinction between public and private prayer. So far, we've only addressed the latter, but there are times in the life of the Church when everyone comes together to pray. This is often part of our liturgy, but it is also an essential component of social prayer, those "prayer meetings" wherein many Christians gather at the same time to pray about the same issues together.

I confess I'm terribly uncomfortable in either setting. My own conversations with God are unguarded, unflinching, and raw. I'm not a very good Christian when I pray. But when it's time for group prayer all I can think is "This is how they will judge me for not being holier."

Prayer meetings tend to feel like private prayers performed in public, so I'm often concerned that these prayers are more about "us" than "him." People grandstand, philosophize, correct, and teach as though God was the one that needed to be changed.

It wouldn't be fair to blame anyone else for my neurosis, but it would also be dishonest not to acknowledge that I have too often been too frank in front of too many.

The results are rarely good.

Consequently, whenever we pray liturgically or socially I feel forced to lie. Or hide. Or put on a good face. But I think it's good practice for me to govern my speech. God wants me to speak with unflinching honesty and impeccable courtesy at the same time, especially given my vocation. So I treat public prayer like a mine field, and I weave through it with rocks in my shoe and one eye covered, holding a puppy eager to pee.

Public prayer is how the church prays. There is no such thing as a solitary Christian—not according to the Second Testament. Church is plural. The Church, corporately, is the Bride of Christ. Which means we've all got a responsibility to belong to the Church, to participate in the Church, and to make the Church holy.

Which means our Church has to pray, and we have to pray as part of it.

My advice is to focus on God and not on the praying. Focus on Christ and not on the other pray-ers. Invite the Spirit to speak to you *en masse* in much the same way as you would invite the Spirit to speak with you privately. Don't be shy. Pray fervently and vocally. Agree with those gathered around you.

Get comfortable carrying the puppy.

> Oh, if I could only pray the way this dog watches the meat! All his thoughts are concentrated on the piece of meat. Otherwise

he has no thought, wish, or hope.
- Martin Luther[51]

I grew up in a church where we often prayed in groups, out loud, simultaneously. Some have referred to this as "Korean Prayer," but I just thought of it as prayer meeting. People would take turns trumpeting above the chatter, which we referred to as "leading out in prayer." Only later did I learn that this sort of prayer was uncommon in the West. Most Mainline, Liturgical, or conservative Evangelical traditions govern prayer like a U.N. Summit: one at a time, in order, preferably rehearsed and doctrinally sound. It took some time for me to adjust to "politician's prayers," and even more to appreciate the call-and-response style of prayer common in European churches. But I've grown fond of them all, in their own way, and I believe it's healthier to have made my peace with the multiplicity of approaches rather than trying to defend my own (which I didn't always enjoy in the first place).

Another distinct feature of my upbringing was the Charismatic understanding of a personal prayer language, more commonly called "speaking in tongues" (though I prefer the term "praying in the Spirit"). Many have lampooned this practice, and many more doubt its legitimacy. I don't want to debate the issue, so let it suffice to say that my own biblical investigations and experiences[52] have settled any theological misgivings I might once have had. I have some criticisms of the Pentecostal movement at large, but consider this a lover's quarrel. For better or worse, I'm one of them.

At first I struggled with mentioning this issue altogether. In some ways it feels like a distraction from a beginner's primer on how to pray comfortably with God. Neither is praying in the Spirit an especially common practice in the church where I currently serve (nor am I likely to make it so). I'm unsure how to help others best experience this gift, and it often feels like I've got a lot to undo before I can ever help someone construct a healthy understanding of what it is and how it works. But I find greater comfort, strength, peace, and clarity when I pray in the Spirit. There have been many times when I was at a loss and could not imagine continuing ministry, marriage, or even life if it weren't for God's gracious gift of allowing me to pour out my heart in a language no one but God understands. I am hard-pressed to consider any more essential skill in my relationship with the Lord than this cocktail of rejuvenation and detoxification. So while I won't delve too deeply here into the baptism of the Holy Spirit and speaking in tongues, allow me to say I hope to later write more eloquently about how others might share in the experience. In the meantime, I won't defend the practice, but simply continue it. I mention it because maybe you practice, too, and it's nice to know you're not the only weirdo in Oz.

> To hunger and thirst after righteousness [means] nothing in the world can fascinate us so much as being near God.
> - Smith Wigglesworth[53]

There are other groups of prayer common among Christians. One way to help yourself get into the habit of daily focused time with God is to find a prayer buddy. Just knowing someone else is going to ask if you prioritized conversation with God tends to help us do so. Prayer is also a frequent occurrence in satellite groups or Bible studies, where small groups of Christians gather to focus on their spiritual development. These can be especially intimidating times of prayer, so I recommend only those who feel comfortable praying do so, and also that those who feel especially comfortable praying keep their prayers brief. There is nothing more disparaging to someone mustering the courage to pray out loud than the person who will not stop praying out loud.

If you feel like you are especially in need of help and strength, it is appropriate to ask other believers to pray for you. My one caution in this regard is to avoid blanket requests, so common on social media and often phrased with a flair for the dramatic ("OMG life is so crazy you guys, I can't believe it. Prayers please!"). These kinds of pleas may be effective once or twice (meaning, others feel like they've got to pray, not that the prayers are especially powerful), but it's easy to fall into the trap of posting like this frequently. If you do this, beware of exhausting your friends and depleting their goodwill. Much like someone who perpetually pouts at a party, the friend who is perpetually "going through a difficult time" gets old fast.

I also think we should be wary of the prayer-guilt via email or social media. The same people who feel

confident proclaiming "If you love the Lord Jesus,
you will repost this and tag ten friends" tend to be the
ones who feel confident wearing enough makeup to
paint a Ronald McDonald house, pet strangers' babies
at Target, and buy antique deer-hunting supplies from
QVC. Our reluctance to participate in their prayer
scams has far less to do with our affection for Jesus
Christ than our fear that their spiritually-diseased
veneration might be contagious.

There may be times when you feel as though God is
directing you to pray for someone else. If you think
about someone, send them a text; if you text them,
pray for them. My friend John does this, and there are
no shortage of times when he's caught someone "at
just the right moment" and been able to offer timely
counsel, encouragement, or friendship.

Sometimes, you may feel as though you're supposed
to ask for someone's permission to pray with them.
This can be awkward, but the best way forward is the
simplest. Just ask: *May I pray for you?* It will seem out
of place, but excessive explanation will only intensify
the strangeness. And in my experience, most people
are far less reluctant to receive prayer than they are to
engage in religious conversation. Prayer seems sweet,
and praying for others in our contemporary, multi-
ethnic and pluralistic culture is often interpreted in
the same light as receiving a blessing. My friend Jim
Mueller describes this kind of prayer as "giving love
away," such that when we lay our hands on each other
and pray sincerely, it feels as though the love flows
freely between us.

> Go where your best prayers take you.
> - Frederick Buechner[54]

Whenever we pray for others, it's called intercession. Intercessory prayer involves our participation in closing the gap between another's reality and their blessed wellbeing. We pray "in the gap" for those that need healing, for those that need protection, for those that need rescue or deliverance or wisdom. The gap can be anything, and we can add our prayers to those of others, believing that a three-cord strand is not easily broken (Ecclesiastes 4.12; 2 Corinthians 1.11; 1 Timothy 2.1).

How do we pray for others, especially when we're either ignorant of what they need or are nowhere close to them physically? The same way we pray anything else. We just bring it to God. God isn't limited by distance, by time zone, or even by our ignorance. God isn't limited at all, so we pray and trust that God is already working toward a solution and our prayers are like little agreements that mean a lot to our loved ones, and therefore a lot to God, also. Does that mean they have no effect on the outcome? No. Outcomes are complex issues that we rarely understand. But prayer changes things, and not just us, but the world and everything in between. There's no telling how or why God answers some prayers the way we want, so every prayer is a "Hail Mary—get your son!" and if we don't get what we want, we trust that he'll help us figure out how life will continue regardless.

If someone asks you to pray, or informs you of a
troubling circumstance, do not promise them you will
pray. Just pray. Right away. With them, there, in that
moment. You will bless them immeasurably more
by taking time right away than you will with your
assurance that later, at a more convenient time, you
will pray. Plus, you'll probably forget to do it later;
or, they'll assume you'll forget, which amounts to the
same thing. So don't delay praying. Just pray.

> The sovereign cure for worry is prayer.
> - William James[55]

I wrote about praying before meals in *The Church
Survival Guide*, and I stand by my earlier assertion
that "Prayer before meals is a good reminder that
everything we have is a gift from God." Likewise, I
maintain that taking "the opportunity to bless the
hands of those who prepare our meals [creates] a
house full of love and respect, peace and honor."[56]
Mealtime prayer is also a good way to conclude each
work day and begin life at home with those we love,
and even though it may sometimes feel rote, we still
benefit from the reminder that God is present and we
are transformed through gratitude.

That said, I go through seasons where I cannot
imagine anything more miserable than praying before
dinner. During those times, I give myself permission
to skip mealtime prayer since I don't have the
bandwidth to sort out my maladjusted thinking. To
clarify, it's never that I feel ungrateful, only that I feel
constrained or judged or pressured to put on a good

show for whoever might be watching. And prayer shouldn't feel like that. And I don't want to submit to those feelings. But I'm such a head-case that I know there are times when I can't fully push off those expectations, anxieties, or frustrations and the better way forward is to temporarily skip a prayer I don't mean for an occasion in which I am already praising God.

> I hate praying before meals. I hate the false
> formality of it. I hate the pretend thanks—as
> though we wouldn't be eating anything at
> all if not for our insistence on lobbing God
> a compliment. But I LOVE praying during
> meals. I love it when the food is so good that
> I'm compelled to say, "Thank you God" and
> I love it when I lurch into praise, exclaiming,
> "I'm so happy right now! This is fantastic."
> Didn't you know that was prayer?
> - *The Adventure of Happiness*[57]

We mentioned two kinds of public prayer—liturgical and social—but there is a third, albeit less common. There is prayer that happens publicly but non-socially; private prayer, in a public space. When I was in high school, for example, there was an annual event during which all Christian students came to stand at the foot of our flag and ask God to guide our country. None of us spoke to each other, praying quietly within the same vicinity but never together. And yet we were together. We were sharing the same space, sharing the same concerns, and sharing participation in the divine life. But we couldn't hear each other, and that made the experience different somehow. I was praying. My friends were praying. We were unified in our prayers, but none of us were talking. Consequently, there was none of the awkwardness associated with "getting it right" or being judged.

This isn't any holier than liturgical or social prayer, though it might be preferable for some. I mention it because it's distinct, though rare, and I crave distinction. I enjoy unique experiences, just as I enjoy crafting those experiences for others to encounter God in a fresh expression.

This is what has led us, at Westwinds Church in Michigan, to create a contemplative prayer garden along our five-acre lawn at the front of our property. We invited seven teams of architects, engineers, artists, and liturgists to construct temporary chapels that would facilitate space for our people to pray. Each chapel is roughly a ten foot cube, set apart by a winding path occupying the green. We call it "The Garden Path." For more information, including pictures, visit: www.facebook.com/ WestwindsGardenPath/.

Here is the sign that welcomes visitors:

> *When someone "walks down the garden path," we understand that they have abandoned God, much like Adam and Eve in Eden. But before Adam and Eve strayed, they strolled. The garden path was always meant to connect us with God, and it was only our rebellion that led us astray. But the way out is also*

the way back—to God, and to our true selves as his shadows. If we want to know God, we have to return to the garden.

This is the path.

PROFILE
SMITH WIGGLESWORTH
ENGLAND
1859-1947

Smith Wigglesworth was a British plumber who had been miraculously healed of appendicitis. As a result, he began to investigate miracles, healings, and the ministry of the Holy Spirit. He was a pioneer in early Pentecostalism, a provocative preacher, and a lightning rod of controversy.

> God never intended his people to be ordinary or commonplace. His intentions were that they should be on fire for him, conscious of his divine power, realizing the glory of the cross that foreshadows the crown.
> - Smith Wigglesworth[58]

Wigglesworth's approach was revolutionary, but his theology was commonplace. As a Methodist, he studied the teachings of John Wesley and had a strong appreciation for the centrality of scripture in the lives of Christians. He maintained that everything he preached, prayed, or performed was rooted in the power of the Spirit as substantiated by the Word.

> The Bible is the Word of God: supernatural in origin, eternal in duration, inexpressible in

valor, infinite in scope, regenerative in power,
infallible in authority, universal in interest,
personal in application, inspired in totality.
Read it through, write it down, pray it in, work
it out, and then pass it on. Truly it is the Word
of God. It brings into man the personality
of God; it changes the man until he becomes
the epistle of God. It transforms his mind,
changes his character, takes him on from
grace to grace, and gives him an inheritance in
the Spirit. God comes in, dwells in, walks in,
talks through, and sups with him.
- Smith Wigglesworth[59]

If you want to pray like Smith Wigglesworth, the first
and most important lesson is this: don't worry about
how you pray, but to whom. If you can't touch the
people, see the people, or even know where the people
for whom you are praying reside, who cares? God is
all that matters. God is the one who spurs us toward
prayer. God is the one who hears our prayers. God is
the one who answers our prayers. God is the one most
invested in our lives after we have completed praying.

Don't concern yourself with technique, but with the
authority of Almighty God, and pray until something
happens.

DID YOU TEST THE EXERCISE?

Yes!

No.

WAS IT HELPFUL?

Yes!

No.

Partly...

WOULD YOU REPEAT IT?

Yes!

No.

Notes:

ACTIVE PRAYER EXERCISE

Stand at the edge of a lake or a pond and gather stones. Hold each stone in your hand and pray over it. These may be prayers of frustration or anger. These may be prayers asking God to help you release an unhealthy attachment. These may be prayers for the welfare of your children. Once you have marked the stones in prayer, skip them across the surface of the water. Let the experience release you as you release your concerns to God.

DID YOU TEST THE EXERCISE?

Yes!

No.

WAS IT HELPFUL?

Yes!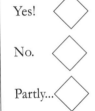

No.

Partly...

WOULD YOU REPEAT IT?

Yes!

No.

Notes:

CONTEMPLATIVE PRAYER
EXERCISE

Basil Pennington, in his book *Centering Prayer*, describes this ancient Christian practice as a means of "putting aside of all the debris that stands in the way of our being totally present to the present Lord, so that He can be present to us."[60] It is a kind of meditation, and can be experienced through four simple steps:

1. **Sit** comfortably with your eyes closed, relax, and quiet yourself. Be in love and faith to God.
2. Choose a sacred **word** that best supports your sincere intention to be in the Lord's presence and open to God's divine action within you.
3. Let that word be gently **present** as your symbol of your sincere intention to be in the Lord's presence and open to God's divine action within you.
4. Whenever you become aware of anything (thoughts, feelings, perceptions, images, associations, etc.), simply return to your sacred word, your **anchor**.

CENTERING PRAYER

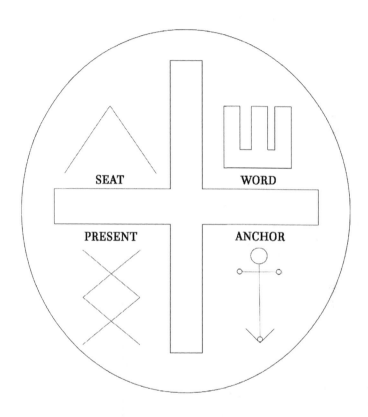

HACK

KOREAN-STYLE PRAYER

By all accounts, this style of prayer originated in the Korean Assembly of God churches, though it has now become widely practiced. In short, it involves large groups of people praying out loud simultaneously along a unified theme. Participants are encouraged to speak at a normal volume and not to worry about the other people around them—either about what their "neighbors" might be praying, or about their neighbors' opinions of their own prayers. This instruction is given to assist participants in overcoming their natural reluctance to talk out of turn, but most would acknowledge that one significant benefit of Korean prayer is the awesome experience of hearing so many people praying together. The combined effect has sometimes been called a "prayer orchestra," where each voice is an instrument played for God's pleasure.

To begin, gather Christians together and have a leader give the instructions above. Then, the leader should supply a topic for prayer with one or two key points to consider. For example, the leader might suggest that we pray for the wellbeing of our city, and that might include racial reconciliation, cessation of violence, and greater investment by fathers in the lives of their children.

Once the topic has been supplied, prayer can begin. It will likely begin with timidity, though confidence will increase. After a few minutes, or whatever length of time feels appropriate, the leader can supply a new topic.

PRAYING THE SCRIPTURES

1 TIMOTHY 2

Most of our biblical prayer exercises have been focused on private prayer, but here I've elected to adapt a portion of St. Paul's letter to Timothy for public use.

> I urge, then, first of all, that petitions, prayers, intercession and thanksgiving be made for all people—for kings and all those in authority, that we may live peaceful and quiet lives in all godliness and holiness. This is good, and pleases God our Savior, who wants all people to be saved and to come to a knowledge of the truth. For there is one God and one mediator between God and mankind, the man Christ Jesus, who gave himself as a ransom for all people. This has now been witnessed to at the proper time. And for this purpose I was appointed a herald and an apostle—I am telling the truth, I am not lying—and a true and faithful teacher of the Gentiles.
> **1 Timothy 2.1-7, NIV**

Here is how I would pray this:

> *Lord we lift up our President, our Governor, our Mayor, and our council to you. We ask that you would make them competent idealists. Purify their desires and guide their actions. Let them know your people are praying for them, and that our desire is to*

see their government flourish insofar as they cooperate with you to heal the world. We ask that you would purify our desires also, that we would govern ourselves in peace and cultivate lives of godliness and holiness, at work and at home, both in our hearts and in our business. We want to please you, and we want to assist others in finding you and knowing you. Thank you for the energy and the passion to do this, and we pray that our own energies and passions would not steer us sideways from your purpose. Help us be honest and full of character, faithful and commendable in the sight of all.

Amen.

YOUR PRAYER:

DATE:

WHY WE'RE STILL SO BAD AT PRAYER

> *As a young Christian I used to pray over and over again, "Oh God, make me strong. Help me to resist temptation." God finally spoke to me one night and said, "You're not going to become strong … ever … John, just how strong do you want to become, seeing you can do nothing without me?"*
> *- John Wimber[61]*

Why does prayer feel like golf?

I've invested so much time, so much devotion, and developed so little competence in return. I've been praying daily for forty years and often wonder why I'm still so bad at it.

It shouldn't be this hard.

But we can't be good at prayer. Not if we understand what prayer truly is. Can we be good at enjoying our wives? Good at laughing spontaneously with friends? It seems manic to imagine sitting across from someone you love, anticipating that they might say something interesting, and then overreacting when they do, only to take over the conversation once more.

This is why Orthodox Bishop Kallistos Ware has reframed prayer, not as something we initiate, but as something we share. "Prayer is not something I do, but something that God does in me," he says. "Prayer is God."[62] And if there are times when we feel like our prayers are good, the danger then becomes arrogance. We will feel as though we have achieved something, which misses the point entirely.

Prayer isn't like fitness or design. You pray to get better—not at praying, but at being you. At being God's. Boston college professor Peter Kreeft says "prayer is like gardening," but in this case we're growing something "alive for eternity." The work is gradual and invisible, but "it is the difference between life and death."[63]

Prayer is how we grow up into ourselves. There is a clock that only ticks when we pray, and it tracks our metamorphosis from sinner to saint.

There are times when, as St. Paul declares in his letter to the church in Rome, "we don't know what to pray, or how" (Romans 8.26), so we depend on God's Spirit to help.

Sometimes we don't even have the strength to say anything at all. That's okay. Take your exhaustion and futility to God. Flop it down in front of the cross. Sigh. Moan. Gaze off into space. However your emptiness manifests, aim it to God, for there is tremendous difference between sitting on the sofa, depressed, and sitting on the sofa, depressed-in-prayer. There is no end to the former, but in the latter scenario our depression is gathered up as an offering to God. This may be one small part of why St. John's *Revelation* is so crucial—his vision of the angels collecting our prayers in bowls, spraying them through heaven reminds us that everything we offer to God is quickened (Revelation 5). All our hopelessness, when aimed at heaven, fills up the bowls that satisfy the Lord.

This isn't to suggest that prayer will be effortless, or even that we will be aware of the effect our prayers have upon the Almighty. It is possible, for example, to sense a roadblock in our prayers. That's what John of the Cross refers to as the "Dark Night of the Soul." But don't focus on your perceptions of prayers. Just pray. The less you think about praying—and all its associated hiccups—the healthier you'll be, since one of the chief obstacles to meaningful prayer is over-concentration. So just pray. It's enough, and your feelings and experiences of prayer will resolve over time.

There are some things that are too precious to entrust to our precarious feelings, so get into the habit of prayer. I eat whether I am motivated by a swell of enthusiasm or whether I am simply in between meetings. It would be foolish to let my lack of exuberance be the controlling factor for my diet. Or my job. Or my time with my family. Some things are so important, we treat them as a matter of course.

Prayer, like antibiotics, cannot be left to chance. We must medicate, whether or not we recognize the urgency.

> Some things are too difficult to be left up to spontaneous desire—things like telling people that we love them, or praying to God. So we do them 'out of habit.'
> - Stanley Hauerwas[64]

Like our feelings, our thoughts require some management and there are skills we can learn within prayer to manage distraction. Buddhists refer to the fleeting thoughts of our anxious selves as the "monkey mind." The mistake we make when we catch our monkey running is we try to subdue it. This is rarely successful. Instead of calming our thoughts, this only increases our anxieties, since we are now anxious about the fact that we are not calmer during prayer. The best way to deal with distraction is simply to realize you've been distracted and return to prayer. That's it. Don't beat yourself up. Don't wallow. Don't make plans or initiate strategies for avoiding distraction next time. Just go back to prayer, leading your wandering mind like a child.[65]

Prayer is like riding a bicycle. We learn to ride by falling off. We stay upright by becoming increasingly aware of our bodies and our balance. We make minute adjustments that allow us to keep moving. The only way we know we need to correct is because we've previously skinned our knees. So pray, and when you get distracted, don't worry that you might lose your balance. Just lift your head and keep pedaling.

Many Christians choose to fast in order to intensify their focused time with God. Fasting involves giving up sustenance (usually all food and drink, except water; though you may customize your fast however you choose) in order to increase your dependence on God. Fasting is healthy, normal, and has been lauded for its effects on our relationship with our Creator.

I do, however, think it's interesting that we only have one recorded instance of Jesus fasting. So, whenever people get overly eager about fasting (or especially judgmental towards those who have never tried it), I like to remind them that Jesus' critics condemned him for "eating and drinking" too heartily (Matthew 11.19).

Like so many issues associated with prayer, the point is not to pursue *this* or *that* activity, but to employ those activities in pursuit of God. Fasting is good, so long as it brings us closer to God. Based on my experience, it almost always does, so I feel comfortable recommending it with just this one caveat: don't let the experience of spiritually-motivated suffering turn you into a jerk. You can't act like a martyr and then complain when no one enjoys your company.

> Most of the great books on prayer are written by experts—monks, missionaries, mystics, saints. I've read scores of them, and mainly they make me feel guilty.
> - Philip Yancey[66]

What about meditation? Should we do that instead of pray? I realize this seems like an innocent question, but it's rather like asking whether I should go for a run or go for a swim. Both activities will burn calories, increase endorphins, and benefit your heart. Likewise, both prayer and meditation will remove your sinful desires, increase your sense of God's presence, and benefit your heart as you become like your Creator; so, do what you love.

Sometimes it helps us to close our eyes. Sometimes it helps us to bow our heads. Sometimes it helps us to raise our face toward the clouds. But there are few rules about prayer. Mainly, we do what helps for as it long as it helps. Because prayer isn't about getting it right, but about becoming increasingly right with God. The paradigm is relational, not aspirational; we become companions, not experts.

For example, there are some benefits, but no requirements, to having a place to pray. Having a set place allows you to more quickly get into the right frame of mind for focused time with God, and your expectations concerning that time can be managed more easily. Prayer is more comfortable when it is more familiar, and a prayer place can help. However, despite the fact that Jesus recommends a "prayer closet" (Matthew 6.6), this is not a command, but rather a warning against praying for show.

Because prayer involves us, anything that helps us get centered on God is both useful and revelatory. So if kneeling or speaking aloud, or making the sign of the cross, or repeating memorized words helps, then do it. I'm not convinced these have any effect on God, but since they do have an effect on how we think, feel, behave, and believe, such postures and practices are worth noting. Bishop Tom Wright agrees, saying "We have learnt a lot in our generation about what we call body language; have we thought about applying it to our prayer?"[67]

Of course, there are times when prayer is intense. Rich. Amazing. When the experience of God is euphoric. When you cannot contain your emotions, and your spirit transcends any competing high. If you've never had such an encounter, you will. Once you do, you'll be changed forever. And since the quality of our experience always works in tandem with the quantity of our time alone with God, my best advice is just to keep praying and not worry too much about it. It's like losing your virginity. It'll happen, just don't rush it.

But on the far side of euphoria is dejection. This, too, will occur. You'll feel like your prayers are going nowhere and God is disinterested in everything you say, anything you request, and the sum total of who you are.

Welcome to the suck—population: you.

Here again, don't stress. Prayer isn't designed for your enjoyment but for your development. And remember, prayer isn't a thing you're meant to perform, but a tether to the power making you God's. So if it doesn't always feel good, that might just mean it's working. It might mean there are some things inside you that don't want to leave, and the heaviness you experience in prayer results from the Spirit of God pressing upon your pride or entitlement or consumptive impulses. They're stubborn, so the Spirit presses more and more and more until all that's left is what God desires to retain.

In the end, our past experience of prayer can only serve as a rough guide for the future. If we cling too tightly, we miss what God has prepared for this moment.

> God shows us new facets of his glory, but we refuse to look at it because we're still searching for the old ones ... Leave the bulbs alone, and the new flowers will come up. Grub them up and hope, by fondling and sniffing, to get at last year's blooms and you will get nothing.
> - C.S. Lewis[68]

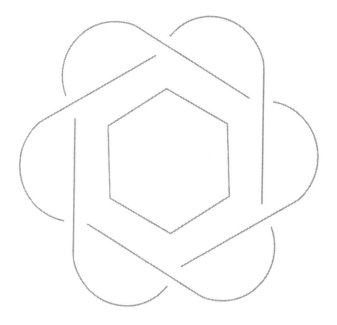

PROFILE

JULIAN OF NORWICH
ENGLAND
1342-1416

JOHN OF THE CROSS
SPAIN
1542-1591

I'm selecting two important pray-ers, since Julian and John both were brilliant, painful, and crazy.

Julian's experience of God resulted in ecstasy but began with a horrifying vision of Christ bleeding to death on the cross. Once she delved into the mystery of her vision, she arrived at her "revelation of divine love."

> I saw no wrath except on man's side, and He forgives that in us, for wrath is nothing else but a perversity and an opposition to peace and to love.
> - Julian of Norwich[69]

John went through a "dark night of the soul" when monks held him captive, during which time he begged God for both physical and spiritual relief. He received neither, until he finally managed to escape from prison on his own.

> Love consists not in feeling great things but in having great detachment and in suffering for the Beloved. The soul that is attached to anything, however much good there may be

in it, will not arrive at the liberty of
Divine Union. For whether it be as
a strong wire rope or a slender and
delicate thread that holds the bird, it
matters not, it it holds really fast; for
until the cord be cut, the bird cannot
fly.
- John of the Cross[70]

How can you pray like these two? Why
would you want to? Both were subjected to
psychological horror before being treated to
their remarkable insights. Nevertheless ...

- Your pain can be redeemed. The
sooner you relinquish your identity
as a victim and reclaim your identity
as God's child, the sooner you can
repurpose your pain to help others.
**Pray that God would give you the
strength to reconstitute
your pain as ministry.**

- Take today's steps without unnaturally
fretting about their misfortunes
or elevating their significance.
**Pray yourself closer to heaven,
visualizing every word as an inch
forward.**

- Both Julian and John spent
considerable time in their latter years
helping others move forward in
their relationship with Christ. **Pray
that you might be given such
opportunity, and that you might
not squander it.**

**DID YOU
TEST THE
EXERCISE?**

Yes!

No.

**WAS IT
HELPFUL?**

Yes!

No.

Partly...

**WOULD YOU
REPEAT IT?**

Yes!

No.

Notes:

ACTIVE PRAYER
EXERCISE

Consider walking a prayer labyrinth. A labyrinth differs from a maze in that a labyrinth has only one path and it leads to the center, and then back out to the margin. The path symbolizes going inward with ourselves under the guidance of God, and then God leading us back out into the world. There are many famous labyrinths, but you don't need anything fancy in order for the experience to be meaningful. You could simply scrawl one on the pavement with chalk, or print one off the Internet, or trace the image along the screen of your phone.

PRAYER LABYRINTH

DID YOU TEST THE EXERCISE?

Yes!

No.

WAS IT HELPFUL?

Yes!

No.

Partly...

WOULD YOU REPEAT IT?

Yes!

No.

Notes:

CONTEMPLATIVE PRAYER
EXERCISE

One of my favorite means of focusing during prayer is to pray with a candle. When I realize my mind has wandered, I'll blow the candle out and relight it. If you do this with other people around you, expect to get the giggles. It's funny, and fun, to see how flawed our attentions truly are.

In the beginning, I recommend trying this for five to seven minutes. If you find the experience useful, you might try to outlast a tea light. But, be warned, the more expensive tea lights can last for up to six hours!

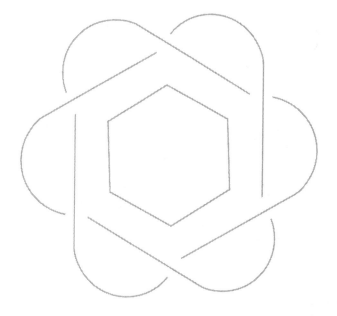

HACK

SAYING AND DOING

When our prayers become discordant, it's best to return to basics. The only way to navigate complexity is with simplicity, and there is no simpler prayer than asking: *Lord, what are you saying to me?* And the follow up question is equally plain: *What do you want me to do about what you're saying?*

Try this for ten minutes a day, for seven days, while recording your thoughts.

PRAYING THE SCRIPTURES

PSALM 23

One of the most famous prayers in scripture is David's
Psalm 23. It is a perfect passage with which to pray.

> The Lord is my shepherd, I shall not want.
>   He makes me lie down in green pastures,
> he leads me beside quiet waters,
>   he refreshes my soul.
> He guides me along the right paths
>   for his name's sake.
> Even though I walk
>   through the darkest valley,
> I will fear no evil,
>   for you are with me;
> your rod and your staff,
>   they comfort me.
> You prepare a table before me
>   in the presence of my enemies.
> You anoint my head with oil;
>   my cup overflows.
> Surely your goodness and love will follow me
>   all the days of my life,
> and I will dwell in the house of the Lord
>   forever.
>
> **Psalm 23**

Here's how I would pray this:

> *God—you've given me everything I need. More
> importantly, you've enabled me to enjoy it and to
> perceive your hand in providing it. Every day, you
> show me some new means by which I am rejuvenated.*

*You've made me boyish without allowing me to be
infantile, and that feels like great fun.*

*Please continue to lead and correct me. It is your
goodness that gives me confidence when I wade into
life's sewers. You're with me in the ER. You're with
me at night in the dark with grieving families. You're
with me when I'm alone.*

*Please reward my noble ambition with more of you.
I can see the way ahead, and your love gives me hope
that better days approach; which is incredible, since
these days are already sweet.*

Amen.

YOUR PRAYER:

DATE:

WE
BECOME
THE
ANSWER
TO
OUR
PRAYERS

The Word of God addressed to us always presupposes the Word of God within us ... How can we hear God's Word? Because we are in God's Word.
- Hans Urs von Balthasar[71]

One of the most common, and yet most puzzling, questions people ask concerns God's will for their lives. Is it God's will for me to get married? Is it God's will for me to marry Susan? Is it God's will for me to stay married to Susan even though she's mean? Is it God's will for me to continue paying Susan child support even though she spends it on cigarettes? Is it God's will for Susan to mysteriously disappear?

We have this impression that God's will is very, very specific and that if we deviate from it we will somehow be cursed. But I suspect that we also want to know whether or not something is "God's will" because then we bear no responsibility for it.

Most of the time we know exactly what God wants; we just need strength to do it. That strength is found in prayer.

I am often asked if it's God's will for someone to get divorced. Usually, before I can respond at all, the person asking follows up with "I know God hates divorce, but in this case ..." Why do we spend so much time asking God to give us a different answer than he gives everyone else? Relationships are difficult; so, work harder at cultivating them, mending them, and forgiving them.

God's will is never that you should avoid difficulty for the sake of your comfort. God's will is never that you should defy scripture in order to make life easier.

What God wants from us results in what God wants for us. God wants obedience, and obedience will result in blessing. Not always. Not without interruption. But in the great majority of circumstances—and certainly over time—when we live the way God intends we get to enjoy life the way God designed it: as a festival of pleasures, wonders, and enjoyments.

Wisdom dictates that you avoid making foolish decisions. If Susan is mean, don't marry her. But godliness requires that you endure the effects of those decisions with grace. Now that you're stuck with Susan, focus less on what a miserable wife she is and learn how to become a remarkable husband so, at least, your children will have one good parent. Also, stop complaining about your wife. The more you proclaim her flaws, the more we're likely to believe that Susan is the one who married an idiot.

> What are the actual demons we must
> exorcize? Grandiosity, loneliness, unbridled
> sexuality, paranoia, woundedness, joylessness
> … this is how Satan comes to us today.
> - Ronald Rolheiser[72]

Many people will discuss the difference between God's general and specific will. Those are helpful terms, to a point. God's general will refers to all the good teaching in the Bible about how we should live—faithfully, generously, in fidelity and love, with integrity. If you want to know God's will, read the Second Testament with a special focus on the gospels and St. Paul's epistles. God's specific will, on the other hand, refers to what God wants from us in particular situations at particular places during particular times. Here, though, a few things must be said.

God's will has great latitude. In the strictest sense, God has no preference for who you marry (or if you marry at all), what job you take, or how many children you have.

For example, when I took the job at the church where I currently serve, I felt like God was speaking to me. I felt like he was saying, "This is a wonderful church where you will have tremendous fun. You'll learn. You'll grow. You'll make lasting friendships. There are some unique challenges, and you'll be far from your family, but this will be great!" And yet I also felt God saying, "Of course, you could take one of the other opportunities available. You could start a new church at home. That would be good, too. You'd grow in different ways, but you would make a wonderful gift to that community."

Do you see what I mean about God's "specific" will? It's not that specific. It's not even that willful. Does God, sometimes, speak to us about these issues? Absolutely. But for the most part, when we ask God about his preferences we must imagine him looking back at us, saying "Well, it's your life, what seems best to you?"

In my case, God was telling me the opportunity I chose was a great one, but there were other great ones, also. Common sense and wise counsel had allowed me to eliminate a host of other, not-so-great opportunities prior to that, but I've always taken St. Augustine's counsel to heart when he said, "Love God, and do as you will."[73]

The way forward involves wedding our intentions to our actions, such that we perceive ourselves as the hands and feet of God working in the world. With the confidence that comes from being rooted in scripture, surrounded by healthy Christian community, and the assurance that God's spirit is guiding us, we must stop waffling about God's will and begin, instead, to actualize it.

We become the answer to our prayers. God makes us creative, innovative, generative, and resourceful. To depend on God is to realize that God lives in us, that he made us like him, and that to be holy is to see God's image shining through us.

Have you seen a Chinese lantern? It's a paper cube with a candle inside. The brighter the candle, the more translucent the paper. That's what happens with us. The more brightly God burns, the more brightly we shine. And that's the goal—that we would shine brightly with Christ.

> God, without us, will not; as we, without God, cannot.
> - St. Augustine[74]

I have profound disagreements on many issues with noted scholar John Dominic Crossan. Nevertheless, he makes an exceptional point in his book *The Greatest Prayer: Rediscovering the Revolutionary Message of the Lord's Prayer*, when he reprimands us for our inactivity. "You have been waiting for God, while God has been waiting for you," he says. "No wonder nothing is happening. You want God's intervention, while God wants your collaboration. The kingdom is here, but only insofar as you accept it, enter it, live it, and thereby establish it."[75] This, Crossan goes on to assert, is why the disciples were sent out in the manner of Jesus himself—healing, proclaiming, delivering—rather than simply fetching the sick back to Christ so he could do everything himself. Because God's kingdom is less about divine intervention and more about divine-human cooperation.

God prefers cooperation over intervention. Not sure if that holds water? Consider Jesus instructing his disciples that they have to "take up their cross and follow him" (Mark 8.34). That's participation, not mere observation. Consider St. Paul's teaching that we are "transformed from glory to glory" into the image of Christ (2 Corinthians 3.18). That's participation, not mere observation.

We want God to show up and fix things for us, but God wants us to show up so God can fix things through us. We want God to do something, but he's already done something—he's sent us. We are God's response to evil, to poverty, to injustice. God has equipped and ennobled us to do everything he would do if he were standing right here, because he is. In us. What else could it possibly mean for us to be the body of Christ (1 Corinthians 12.12-30), than that our hands are his hands and our minds bear his thoughts?

Did you think it was just a metaphor?

> I used to pray that God would feed the hungry, or do this or that, but now I pray that he will guide me to do whatever I'm supposed to do, what I can do. I used to pray for answers, but now I'm praying for strength. I used to believe that prayer changes things, but now I know that prayer changes us and we change things.
> - Mother Teresa[76]

Can you imagine walking through a city downtown and seeing a young boy, lost, wandering in the middle of traffic? Can you imagine thinking "God, why don't you send someone to rescue him?" Or would you just run out and grab the boy, leading him to safety?

We are the answers to the prayers of others. We are the means through which God plans to heal the world. Prayer is an integral part of how we cooperate with God. It's how we receive our marching orders from him, how we receive the energy to accomplish those instructions, and how we experience the confidence to make adjustments and maintain our sensitivity in the middle of our assignments. Prayer is constant communication with God. Prayer is constant cooperation with God.

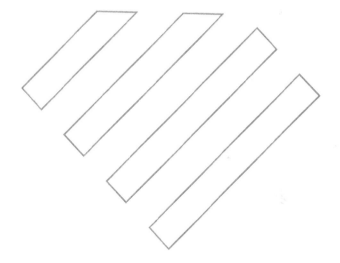

PROFILE

GEORGE MULLER
GERMANY
1805-1898

Muller was the director of the Ashley Down Orphanage in England and provided education to over 120,000 children through his 117 schools. He worked closely with Dwight Moody, preached for Charles Spurgeon, and was a key influence in Hudson Taylor's decision to become a missionary.

Not a bad resume at all.

> I seek the will of the Spirit of God through, or in connection with, the Word of God. The Spirit and the Word must be combined. If I look to the Spirit alone without the Word, I lay myself open to great delusions, also.
> - George Muller[77]

But the real reason I've included Muller is that his ministry was marked by miraculous answers to prayer. Muller had over 50,000 specific recorded answers to prayers in his journals, 30,000 of which he said were answered the same day or the same hour that he prayed them.[78]

If you want to pray like Muller, here's a few pointers:

1. **Pray in, with, and through the Bible**. Muller was famous for finding out what the Bible said about any particular issue— including what the Bible promised to faithful believers—and then he would put his finger on that promise and hold it there while he prayed. Sometimes he would look for days before he found his answer, and only then would he begin praying. Fortunately, we can now use the Internet to search for "scriptures concerning _____" and arrive at sound conclusions much earlier; but I recommend highlighting those passages in your Bible and holding your finger on them regardless, since it helps keep us rooted in the surrounding context.

2. **Meditate on scripture.** Don't just pray it, but consider what it means for you to submit to God's Word. Consider the adventure, the obedience, the requirements, and the passion inherent therein.

**DID YOU
TEST THE
EXERCISE?**

Yes!

No.

**WAS IT
HELPFUL?**

Yes!

No.

Partly...

**WOULD YOU
REPEAT IT?**

Yes!

No.

Notes:

ACTIVE PRAYER EXERCISE

Actives can learn to meditate on scripture using Eugene Peterson's simple four-step method of: reading, thinking, praying, and doing.

Reading involves picking just a few verses of the Bible (two or three will suffice) and reading them over and over for five minutes. You may find it helpful to insert line breaks where there are none, thereby focusing more intensely on the words.

For example, Psalm 119.105 says "Your word is a lamp unto my feet and a light unto my path," which might then be read repeatedly by breaking it up in this way:

> *Your Word*
> *Your Word is a lamp*
> *A lamp unto my feet.*
> *Your Word is a lamp…and a light*
> *A light*
> *A light unto my path.*

Thinking involves asking questions pertaining to what you just read. What does this mean for me? How can I apply this?

What does God intend for me, in this moment, to understand? What have I possibly missed in my life previously that this scripture is meant to correct? How might this help me in the future? Do this for five minutes, also.

Praying means taking the scripture you read and the thoughts upon which you meditated and saying them out loud, asking God for help to live consistently with his Word.

Doing involves getting up and trying, immediately, to perform some action in alignment with all that you've just prayed, thought, and read.

DID YOU TEST THE EXERCISE?

Yes!

No.

WAS IT HELPFUL?

Yes!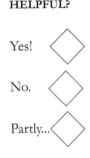

No.

Partly...

WOULD YOU REPEAT IT?

Yes!

No.

Notes:

CONTEMPLATIVE PRAYER
EXERCISE

Contemplatives often enjoy the scriptural method known as *lectio divina* (sacred reading). It is a four-stage process, though each stage tends to flow naturally into the others. It should not be rushed, but it can definitely be enjoyed.

Lectio (reading). Read a short passage of scripture slowly, noticing every word, every phrase, and even the ordering of the dictation. Read it like poetry. Read it like a love letter. Read it as though God were speaking directly, and solely, to you.

Meditatio (meditation). Christian meditation is a scriptural practice (Genesis 24.63; Joshua 1.8; Psalm 1.2; 48.9; 77.3; 119.15; 143.5) wherein we submit to the authority of God and bring our lives in line with his Word. Center on God. Consider all God intends for you to understand based on what you read in the scripture.

Oratio (prayer). Next, take everything you've experienced and offer it up to God as a prayer. Pray the scripture.

Pray your meditation. Invite God to speak to you and change you and challenge you.

Contemplatio (contemplation). Finally, sit in silence. Allow God's presence to wash over you. Relax. Stop striving. Just ... be.

HACK

I.O.U.S

The Psalms give us instructions about how to understand God's Word, and we can use those instructions as a template for how to pray the scripture. Famed pastor John Piper suggests using the acronym IOUS (I-owe-yous) to help us remember the four-step process.

> **Incline** my heart to your testimonies (Psalm 119.36: *Turn my heart toward your statutes and not toward selfish gain*). This means learning to be sensitive and malleable to the scriptures' intent, ready to change and eager to learn.

> **Open** my eyes to see wonderful things (Psalm 119.18: *Open my eyes that I may see wonderful things in your law*). Ask God to show you something that you can use to praise him.

> **Unite** my heart to fear your name (Psalm 86.11: *Teach me your way, Lord, that I may rely on your faithfulness; give me an undivided heart, that I may fear your name*). This means honoring God above all competing concerns, aligning your behaviors with his desires.

Satisfy me in the morning with your steadfast love (Psalm 90.14: *Satisfy us in the morning with your unfailing love, that we may sing for joy and be glad all our days*). Conclude by focusing on the way God's love is revealed in this passage and how praying that love will make you more loving, also.

PRAYING THE SCRIPTURES

THE LORD'S PRAYER

We have very few of Jesus' prayers recorded, but the most famous is undoubtedly the Our Father. Given in response to the disciples' request for instruction in prayer, The Lord's Prayer is the definitive template for how to pray biblically.

> Our Father in heaven, hallowed be your name. Your kingdom come, your will be done, on earth as it is in heaven. Give us this day our daily bread, and forgive us our debts, as we also have forgiven our debtors. And lead us not into temptation, but deliver us from the evil one.
> **Matthew 6.9-13, NIV**

Here's how I would pray this:

> *Lord God, you are my Father. You have claimed me, and also promised to show me how to live—to apprentice me in your holy vocation. Your name is great and powerful. The world is yours, just as heaven is yours, and I want to live in such a way as to make your presence obvious here, like it is there. I want to cooperate with you to heal the world. I want to live as a citizen of your kingdom. Give me what I need, including the power to forgive those I hate. Forgive me, too, since there's no shortage of blemishes on my record. Keep me out of trouble. Give me the wisdom not to place myself in situations where I might be compromised. Keep me pure. Make me good.*
>
> *Amen.*

YOUR PRAYER:

DATE:

THE LORD'S PRAYER

HOLINESS

Be done, the WILL of you ...GUIDE us from temptation

DISTRIBUTION

Be manifest, the KINGDOM of you ...FORGIVE our debts

CREATION

Be holy, the NAME of you ..SUPPLY our bread

OUR FATHER IN HEAVEN...

THE
FAITH
WEB

NINE: THE FAITH WEB

Prayer is the respiratory function of the church;
without it we suffocate and die at last, like a living
body deprived of the breath of life.
- A.W. Tozer[79]

One of my doctoral students from Portland Seminary
is a Lutheran missionary named Scott Ness. In his
research, he concluded that every Christian needs
a "Faith Web" to keep them balanced, healthy, and
growing. Scott's Faith Web[80] describes the network
of relationships surrounding us, including our sages,
protégés, and peers.

- Sages are the people who lead us and stretch
  us, typically men and women of our same
  gender who are several steps ahead in both
  life and faith. They are our mentors, teaching
  us what's next and helping us avoid the pitfalls
  in which they became trapped.

- Protégés are the people to whom we are
  passing on what we know and what we've
  learned.

- Peers are, of course, the people in roughly the
  same stage of life as us, with whom we share
  our experiences.

Scott maintains that the church already provides a
Faith Web for most Christians, but we fail to utilize it.
We're subconsciously aware of what the church is and
what the church is for, but rarely either contribute to
or benefit from the church in the way God intends.

But the simplest, most effective way forward for us to develop in our relationship with God is to invest heavily in existing relationships.

> God's will is like a business check that must be cosigned in order to be validated. The Church is the cosigner, and prayer is our signature.
> - *The Church Survival Guide*[81]

Many of us have confidence that God hears our prayers, but we're never sufficiently certain of his response. Is God speaking to us through our conscience, our impressions, our sense of assurance? Or is it possible the feelings we have reveal our preferences in the matter and we're attributing those to God out of naïveté or self-delusion?

How do we know?

Begin with scripture. That's the resource that keeps us from fabricating nonsense, since we can point back to it and get a clear starting point at least. But scripture is hard to interpret and there are sometimes conflicting scriptures along a certain topic. Forgiveness and justice, for example, are difficult concepts to navigate amid the complexities of ordinary life—we know we are meant to forgive, but does that also mean resuming fellowship with our rapist? Is there any responsibility to pursue justice that others might be protected?

To help, God directs us to the Church, cross-referencing pastors and theologians with fellow Christians and peers in order to ensure we're applying the Bible healthily. God sometimes speaks to us through nonbelievers, using their words and actions to quicken our understanding, thereby giving us new insight into the scriptures (though never, it must be said, in conflict with them). There are other ways God speaks—through circumstances, through "coincidences," through media, etc.—but these are the main ones, in order: through his Word, through his Church, and through his world.

> God looks down from heaven on all mankind
> to see if there are any who understand,
> any who seek God.
> **- Psalm 14.2, NIV**

What is the relationship between prayer and other Christians? Specifically, is it possible to hear God's words in the mouth of someone else? To hear them speaking and immediately know it's God speaking to you, through them?

Of course.

Often when I'm finished preaching I will have people approach me in the lobby and tell me I must have been reading their thoughts, or that the message was just for them. In these cases, it's clear that, though I had no knowledge of these people or their circumstances, God was able to bend my words to his ultimate purpose for his individual children.

Sometimes God speaks to us through common sense. It we ask God whether or not we should buy a lottery ticket, the answer will always be "No." But sometimes God speaks to us through the community of saints called his Church. So if we ask our fellow Christians whether we should sell all our earthly possessions and become a hermit to pray in the woods, they might remind us we have school-aged children, elderly parents, and responsibilities to our employees which would make the "selfless" life of a hermit one of the most selfish decisions imaginable.

My best advice is that if everyone who loves you and loves God tells you you're wrong, stop praying for a different answer. As Tozer said, "Prayer is never an acceptable substitute for obedience."[82]

I cannot tell you how often I wish people took that advice more seriously, so let me repeat it: if they're all telling you you're wrong, you are.

Here is a laundry list of quotes from the last six months of being a pastor. I wish I was exaggerating, but I'm not.

> *We can't cope with the guilt of pre-marital sex, so we're getting married.*

> *Marijuana has proven medicinal properties, and I want my children to be relaxed.*

> *We're not doing anything wrong; just don't tell my wife.*

In all these cases, dozens of loving Christians have come around these people to say:

> *Marriage doesn't solve sexual frustration ...*

> *That's criminal ...*

> *If your wife can't know, you can't continue ...*

But what if our friends are wrong? What if our church is misguided or overly judgmental?

These are valid concerns. However, the time to adjudicate our church is never when our church is challenging our behavior. If you're concerned about the trustworthiness of your church, make a decision about how to handle those concerns when you're not under scrutiny. You should never respond to a question concerning your character with an assault upon the character of those who hold you accountable.

Some, of course, may cite Job's comforters as proof that the community can be wrong. Let me be clear: the community *can* be wrong. Job's comforters were wrong. But that's one story in a Bible that covers roughly 4,000 years. So the odds that the people who are challenging you *right now* are "just like" Job's comforters are slim indeed. Furthermore, Job's comforters were conflating suffering for sin. They concluded that, since Job was suffering, he must have sinned secretly and simply not known about it. That's a very different issue than someone sinning obviously and refusing to acknowledge it, or someone suffering as a result of blatant sin they refuse to address. Job's comforters fabricated sin to justify the suffering, whereas most of us are trying to excuse sin in order to blame our suffering on God.

We all like to say that "everyone sins" and "no one is perfect." But those are much harder to accept when someone is challenging us on our specific behaviors at a particular time.

I say this, by the way, as someone who has often been backed into a corner and come out with my fangs bared. I can tell you that such a defensive posture has rarely served me well, and that the more willing I am to listen to those that love me, the healthier my relationships have become—especially my relationship with God.

Never forget that it is in "repentance and rest" that we find salvation (Isaiah 30.15). We're too afraid of repentance, too wary of being challenged, and altogether too defensive about our behavior.

Let us repent more than we request permission.

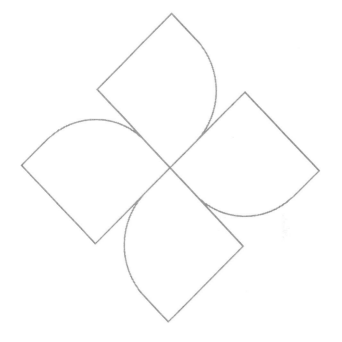

PROFILE

A.W. TOZER
UNITED STATES OF
AMERICA, 1897-1963

Aiden Wilson Tozer was a Christian pastor whose writings have more influentially shaped modern prayer than any other. His book *The Knowledge of the Holy* is still taught in colleges and seminaries all over the world, and I have personally used it as a text for over a dozen courses training pastors.

> It is doubtful God can ever bless a man
> greatly until he has hurt him deeply.
> - A.W. Tozer[83]

If you want to pray like Tozer, you've got to "pray until you pray." That was Tozer's terminology for the common problem that we cease praying before we've truly focused on God. Since our minds wander and our attentions are scattered, most prayer time is really spent trying to wrangle our thoughts. Then, we stop just as we're finally attending to God.

Here are some suggestions:

> If you're pursuing focused time with God,
> **eliminate all the distractions you can**.
> Much like a responsible driver who refuses

178

to text while doing 90 mph on the freeway, a conscientious pray-er will deliberately set aside mental space to concentrate on God.

If you're pursuing focused time with God, **go to a comfortable location and assume a comfortable posture**. There's no use contorting yourself into knots, thereby creating new distractions, only so you can try to eliminate the distractions you've already failed to leave behind.

If you're pursuing focused time with God, **grab a paper and a pen** so you can write down your requests, as well as any insights you might receive. When you look at your blank paper after ten minutes, you'll know you haven't yet begun.

DID YOU TEST THE EXERCISE?

Yes!

No.

WAS IT HELPFUL?

Yes!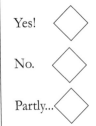

No.

Partly...

WOULD YOU REPEAT IT?

Yes!

No.

Notes:

ACTIVE PRAYER EXERCISE

The easiest way for us to begin experiencing the Faith Web is through conversation. We don't even have to tailor our conversations differently for our sages, protégés, and peers since their responses will differ naturally. Just talk. Pray together. Be open and honest and forthright about your ambitions, challenges, and concerns.

Start with these conversation prompts:

I've been praying about …

What do you think about this situation?

What do you think God might be saying to me through these circumstances?

THE FAITH WEB

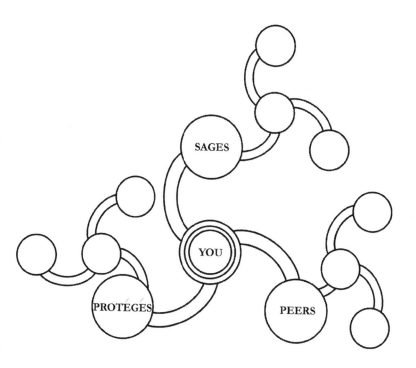

**DID YOU
TEST THE
EXERCISE?**

Yes!

No.

**WAS IT
HELPFUL?**

Yes!

No.

Partly...

**WOULD YOU
REPEAT IT?**

Yes!

No.

Notes:

CONTEMPLATIVE PRAYER
EXERCISE

Contemplatives may take great solace in scribing their Faith Web, either artistically or in bullet form. Sometimes just writing it down gives us a healthier perspective and counteracts feelings of isolation. Sometimes it's helpful to draw or doodle, treating the composition of our Faith Web as a means of centering prayer (or, on a less "spiritual" level, as something akin to an adult coloring book).

Begin with all the sages, protégés, and peers that come to your mind. Then, connect them to one another so you can begin to see the overlapping and complex beauty into which the Lord has placed you.

HACK

METAPHORS FOR DISCERNMENT

My friend Rick Callahan often uses four metaphors to determine what God might be saying to him. I've used these metaphors primarily in the context of leadership, but they are also very useful in prayer and in the process of discernment with other believers.

- Speed bumps are those things in life that constantly slow you down and frustrate your progress. This might be something like an unfamiliarity with scripture, the lack of solid Christian friendships, or a failure to find a place of meaningful service in your local church. **What speed bumps keep slowing you down?**

- Brick walls are obstacles that stop you dead in your tracks, impeding any further progress whatsoever. Sexual misconduct, an absolute refusal to give, or the lack of basic life requirements like somewhere to live or something to eat are all examples of obstacles that mean you cannot move forward in your relationship with God until you address these

184

issues. **What brick walls have stopped you dead in your tracks?**

- Visions are clear mental pictures of how things could be in the future if you stay faithful and God continues to bless your efforts. They are imaginations of life at its optimum, providing us with the energy and confidence to move forward. **What visions has God given you?**

- Mirrors are moments when we see ourselves, warts and all. Sometimes they occur when we catch ourselves doing or saying something awful—something we could never imagine actually doing! When they occur, it's God's way of telling us there is hidden sin that must be excavated. **What mirror moments has God given you?**

When you pray, begin by asking God for clarity about these issues. Write down the impressions you have, asking the Lord to refine and purify your intuition.

PRAYING THE SCRIPTURES

COLOSSIANS 3

Since much of our conversation in this chapter has focused on the relationships among believers, it seems fitting to pray through that same issue as it appears in St. Paul's letters to the Second Testament church.

> As God's chosen people, holy and dearly loved, clothe yourselves with compassion, kindness, humility, gentleness and patience. Bear with each other and forgive one another if any of you has a grievance against someone. Forgive as the Lord forgave you. And over all these virtues put on love, which binds them all together in perfect unity.
> **Colossians 3.12-14, NIV**

Here's how I would pray this:

> *God, you have chosen us—not just me, but all of us together. You have called us holy, even when we were not, and call us now to become saints in truth as well as in name. You love us, and I ask for the strength and the character to love my fellow Christians. Make me compassionate, humble, and patient. I am none of those things without you, and I am barely those things when you are working in me. Please change me. Help me to put up with whatever nonsense comes my way, and to forgive the people who fumble their way through faith. My blindness makes me abrasive,*

inconsiderable, and unkind. Please forgive me. Help me to be more loving, more often, and to work harder at bringing together your sons and daughters as my brothers and sisters.

Amen.

YOUR PRAYER:

....

....

....

....

....

....

....

DATE:

WHAT WE'RE ALLOWED TO PRAY FOR

> *Whatever the theoretical difficulties, we must continue*
> *to make requests of God. And on this point we get*
> *no help from those who keep on reminding us that*
> *this is the lowest and least essential kind of prayer.*
> *They may be right; but so what? Diamonds are more*
> *precious than cairngorms, but the cairngorms still*
> *exist and must be taken into account.*
> *- C.S. Lewis[84]*

It's okay to ask for things.

Jesus asked, in Gethsemene, and "the student is never greater than the master" (Luke 6.40). Of course, Jesus' prayer didn't get answered, but that's okay too, since it reminds us that we don't always get what we want.

Sometimes, what we want isn't best.

After all, Jesus' death was a sacrifice that changed the history of the world. His death was sacred, a witness to the cruel limitations of power and control. His death saved us. Maybe, if he hadn't died, his Father would have launched a back-up plan, or maybe it would have happened several years later, but the point is that you and I have reason to appreciate that his request was declined.

> This, I thought, is what is meant by "thy will be done" in the Lord's Prayer, which I had prayed time and time again without thinking about it. It means that your will and God's will may not be the same. It means there's a good possibility that you won't get what you pray

> for. It means that in spite of your prayers,
> you're going to suffer.
> - Wendell Berry[85]

We all struggle with the question of when it's appropriate to ask for things. We know that mature believers don't pester God with requests. We know that God intends for us to be the answer to our prayers, and to the prayers of others. We know we're meant to be content and to keep our desires in submission to the Spirit. We know that God is our "Savior, not our Santa."[86] And yet the Second Testament still asserts that we should pray (Matthew 6.6-8; Hebrews 4.6) and that prayer should include asking God for help (Luke 13.11; John 14.13-14; 1 John 5.14-15).

At what point can our concerns become acceptable requests to God?

Right away. And without interruption. If it matters to you, it matters to God, but I humbly recommend you place those requests within the right order.

The danger of asking for things in prayer is that we do it too soon, without any of the framework that scripture intends to govern our relationship with God. When we do this—jump straight to the asking without recognizing the One to whom we're praying, or what he's already accomplished, or what he might want to accomplish in and with and through us—we let "greed get in the way of grace."[87]

> More things are wrought by prayer than this
> world dreams of.
> - Alfred, Lord Tennyson[88]

A number of years ago I received word that someone
distantly connected to our church was "demonized."
If you're unfamiliar with the term, it's loosely used
to describe those who believe that bad things are
happening to them because of malevolent spirits.
Those bad things may include sickness, failure, tragedy
or dark thoughts. Though I did not know this person,
they had a reputation, and I was reluctant to visit
(and even doubly reluctant to pray in some misguided
attempt to cast out a devil I wasn't sure was home in
the first place).[89]

Nevertheless, I went and prayed. I didn't try and
correct the person. It wasn't the time. They were
scared and dysregulated. They could hardly breathe.
But after I prayed, they calmed down.

Many pressed me about why I didn't "set them
straight" or tell them it wasn't real, and I responded by
saying, "It's real to them."

A great many things are real to us, and if they are real
to us it is appropriate to bring them to God. God, who
is "gracious and compassionate, slow to anger and rich
in love" (Psalm 103.8), is far more sympathetic than
me, and is capable of handling our needs, however
comparatively insubstantial they may seem.

Do you really need greater financial stability? Maybe not in comparison to the thousands of people starving all over the world. But if you're scared about money, it's no use berating yourself for being afraid. Just pray. Ask God for help. He may calm you down. He may help you find a new job that increases your compensation. He may send someone knocking at your door with an unexpected inheritance. Or he may firmly tell you to get over yourself. But how will you know until you bring it to him in prayer?

> If you go to pray and you are feeling angry, pray anger; if you are sexually preoccupied, pray that preoccupation; if you are feeling murderous, pray murder; and if you are feeling full of fervor, and want to praise and thank God, pray fervor. Every thought or feeling is a valid entry into prayer. What's important is that we pray what's inside of us and not what we think God would like to see inside of us.
> - Ronald Rolheiser[90]

We're afraid to pray, for fear that God will not, or maybe even cannot, honor our requests. But faith is godly imagination, and if you can imagine a cursory way in which God can respond favorably to your noble request, then you must also imagine that God can out-imagine even your best case scenario.

Desire is not evil. Even common desires like a better car or the love of a beautiful woman or the sense that our work matters are not ungodly. At worst, they're neutral. At best, they're neutral. The danger comes when we fixate on our desires, or when the satisfaction of those desires makes us haughty.

> To love is to be transformed into what
> we love. To love God is therefore to be
> transformed into God.
> - John of the Cross[91]

For years I have laid in bed next to my daughter and sung "You are my sunshine." It's the second verse that makes us well up with tears, every time. Does God get tired of our repeated requests? Not any more than Anna and I get tired of crooning "I dreamed I held you in my arms." The connection we feel in prayer is most closely emulated in the bedtime rituals of parents and children. It's that good, for God; and it can be that good for us, too.

God will never make us feel needy, as though he is bothered by our requests. He is not our boyfriend, but our benevolent Father, and he is charmed, rather than crazed, by our petitions.

So pray. Boldly. About everything. Because if it's in you, it's coming to God whether you want it or not. You may as well extend yourself the courtesy of articulating your requests rather than trying to conceal them.

PROFILE

MEISTER ECKHART
GERMANY
1260-1328

There is no more greatly revered mystic in the
Christian tradition than Meister Eckhart. He came to
prominence in a tense season of church history and
worked tirelessly to bring disparate groups together.
He was maligned, attacked, and posthumously revered.
Many scholars see strong similarities between Eckhart
and Thomas Aquinas, as though the two giants were
approaching the same ends, albeit through very
different means.

> The outward work will never be puny if the
> inward work is great.
> - Meister Eckhart[92]

I most appreciate Eckhart's focus on God's
abundance, fruitfulness, and love. That focus on God's
love quickly translates into a compulsion for Christian
action—because God is so loving, we must work to
heal the world.

> The price of inaction is far greater than the
> cost of making a mistake.
> - Meister Eckhart[93]

If you want to pray like Meister Eckhart, you'll need to divest yourself of attachment to things, people, and even of yourself. As Eckhart said, "the more you have, the less you own."

> First, ask God to **release you of your dependence upon your material possessions**, your intellectual resources, and your relational network. To be clear, these things are not evil, but Eckhart maintained that we rely on them too greatly and would be healthier if we relied more substantially on God. Go to God first, and be amazed at how he supplies.

> Second, ask God to **release you of your expectations and demands of others**. Ask God to make you gentler and more patient, less exacting and intolerant. Ask God to reveal those ways you consciously or unconsciously try and control others, or whimper after their affections. Love God first, and wholly, and let all other loves flow out of his love for you.

> Finally, ask God to help you **let go of yourself**. At first blush, this seems silly. How can we stop being ourselves? But the answer is easier and more familiar than you might guess. We are not our own. We belong to God. Like St. Paul we are slaves to Christ and apostles of God. We have no will but his and no ambition than to glorify him. Pray for strength to embody Jesus' words that it is not our will, but God's that should be done.

DID YOU TEST THE EXERCISE?

Yes!

No.

WAS IT HELPFUL?

Yes!

No.

Partly...

WOULD YOU REPEAT IT?

Yes!

No.

Notes:

ACTIVE PRAYER
EXERCISE

The best way to pray about what you want is to write it down and keep it somewhere you'll see it often. I keep many of my hopes and dreams on Post-it® Notes, and when I pray about them I like to hold the note in my hand. After a while, the notes get crumpled and lose their stickiness, so I replace them with new notes and keep the old ones in a scrapbook. There's nothing magical about the process, but it keeps me focused on what I want and reminds me that I need God's help to get it.

There's no more satisfying feeling than taking the final note off my desk for the final time, knowing God has answered my prayer.

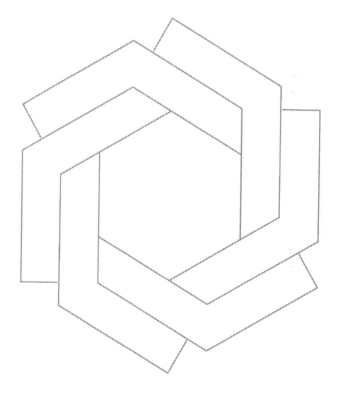

DID YOU TEST THE EXERCISE?

Yes!

No.

WAS IT HELPFUL?

Yes!

No.

Partly...

WOULD YOU REPEAT IT?

Yes!

No.

Notes:

CONTEMPLATIVE PRAYER
EXERCISE

Contemplatives may find it helpful to keep a recollection diary, in which they can gather their requests and re-send them to God.

Such a diary might be highly artistic, wherein the pray-er writes the word HAPPY on a page and decorates it; then, when they pray and ask God to help them experience true happiness, they might trace their finger over that word again and again, as a centering prayer.

Conversely, such a diary might be highly organized, wherein the pray-er keeps a checklist of all requests made and when/if they were answered (complete with timestamp and any associated memos).

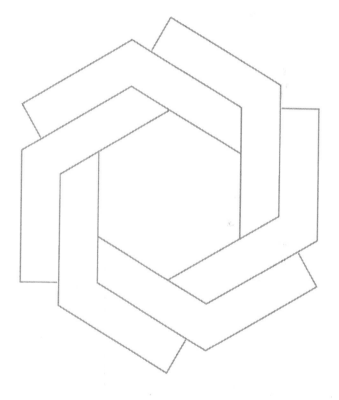

HACK

MY FATHER'S PRAYER

I dedicated this book to my father, who taught me how to pray. More importantly, he taught me that God is good and can be trusted with those prayers. God is not afraid of my emotions, neither is God overly enamored with my wit. He's steadfast, measured, and full of love.

Modern people are increasingly uncomfortable with the understanding of God as our Father. They project onto Father God all the worst sins of patriarchy, imagining God to be misogynistic and oppressive. I can't help but wonder if they've ever met a good man, or if their conception of God might not be healthier if they'd had a father like mine.

Dad taught me there are three components to prayer: thanksgiving, repentance, and request.

> We begin with **thanksgiving**, acknowledging that God has not only blessed us but is also growing our ability to appreciate what we have. God is the source of both our provision and our gratitude. These qualities work in tandem to make us happier, more positive, and more godly.

After praising God, we ask God for mercy and repent of our sins. In the strictest sense, we've already been forgiven for our sins, but the daily practice of **repentance** grows us increasingly into the people God designed us to become. Everything we do, or say, or think that falls outside of God's prescription for healthy living must be named and put off. We must turn away from our sins, over and over again—both in general and in specific ways—and turn toward Christ.

Finally, we bring our **requests** to God. These can be requests of any kind—for healing, for financial stability, for wisdom, for guidance, for relational wellbeing, for success in business, etc. But since God commands us to ask, and tells us he hears, ask away.

PATERNAL PRAYER

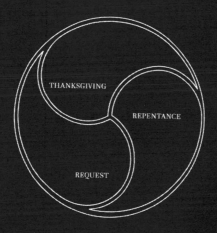

PRAYING THE SCRIPTURES

JAMES 5

We have yet to pray through a scripture that specifically addresses how we ask for things from God. Let us do so now, citing Jesus' brother's letter to the Christian church.

> Is anyone among you in trouble? Let them pray. Is anyone happy? Let them sing songs of praise. Is anyone among you sick? Let them call the elders of the church to pray over them and anoint them with oil in the name of the Lord. And the prayer offered in faith will make the sick person well; the Lord will raise them up. If they have sinned, they will be forgiven. Therefore confess your sins to each other and pray for each other so that you may be healed. The prayer of a righteous person is powerful and effective.
> **James 5.13-16, NIV**

Here's how I would pray this:

God, we bring those that need healing to you. Restore their bodies. Calm their thoughts. Let them know that they're not alone, that your Spirit is with them and you are working to make them whole. We praise you in advance for this, and join together with our elders and church leaders to proclaim we believe you still perform miracles. We believe you can make them well. We believe you can raise them up. In obedience to your word we take a moment now and offer up a confession for our sins. Remove the stain from our souls. Forgive us. We're not perfect. We're not even close. Please help us to live in line with your Word. We thank you again for hearing us, and thank you again for making us righteous and holy by your Spirit.

Amen.

YOUR PRAYER:

....

....

....

....

....

....

....

....

DATE:

DEVELOPING A RULE OF LIFE

May my prayer be set before you like incense; may the lifting up of my hands be like the evening sacrifice …
-King David, in his Book of Psalms

The one heirloom in our family is my mother's grand piano. She bought it for $100 at a flea market, thinking it would serve as an interesting "coffee table." But when she got the piano home, she realized something of great value was hidden under the surface. Mum refurbished the piano, and it now occupies the pride of place in her living room.

My fondest memories of my daughter with her grandmother involve the two of them singing at the bench, banging ivory prayer.

Like that hundred dollar heirloom, there's more value to uncover with prayer. If you read any other titles on the subject, they will cover entirely new material in a wholly different way. Read widely, so you can pray deeply, borrowing insights and practices from the best and godliest.

Now that you've completed this book, the next step is for you to create a rule of life. That term refers to the daily habits and practices you cultivate in order to increase awareness of God's presence, your comfort with him, and your reliance upon his Spirit. Many Evangelicals call this daily devotions, consisting largely of Bible reading and prayer. But a significant number of people find "devotions" problematic, so your task is to go back through the suggested exercises in this book and select a couple that have been especially meaningful.

The important thing to remember is that prayer isn't a chore. God is with you whether you're praying or not, so do what you can to aim your thoughts and heart and intentions toward him without the associated guilt of feeling prayerless. Remember: prayer is like breathing. Remember: we pray to become holy, not because we are. Remember: prayer is not something we do, but something we are.

And no matter what, we are God's.

Dr. David McDonald,
April 27, 2017,
the priory of Westwinds Church, Jackson, Michigan

ENDNOTES

INTRODUCTION: GOD LIKES MY JOKES

1   Heschel, Abraham Joshua, "Abraham Joshua
    Heschel Quotes," *BrainyQuote*, accessed May 11,
    2017, https://www.brainyquote.com/quotes/
    quotes/a/abrahamjos167949.html.

2   Piper, John, *The Pleasures of God: Meditations on
    God's Delight in Being God*, (Multnomah Books:
    New York, 1991), 216.

3   Cohen, Leonard, "Leonard Cohen Quotes,"
    BrainyQuote, accessed May 11, 2017, https://
    www.brainyquote.com/quotes/quotes/l/
    leonardcoh390167.html.

CHAPTER ONE: WE LEARN TO PRAY BY PRAYING

4   A.W. Tozer, as quoted in Seaver, W.L., compiler.
    *Prayer: Communing With God in Everything—Collected
    Insights from A.W. Tozer,* (Moody Publishers:
    Chicago, 2016), 153.

5   Rolheiser, Ronald, *Prayer: Our Deepest Longing,*
    (Franciscan Media: Cincinnati, OH, 2013), viii.

6   Cohen, Leonard, *Book of Mercy*, (McClelland &
    Stewart: Toronto, ON, 1984), 21; my paraphrase.

7   Brother Lawrence, *The Practice of the Presence of God,* trans. John J. Delaney, (Doubleday: New York, 1977), 35.

8   Berry, Wendell, "Prayer Quotes," *BrainyQuote,* accessed May 11, 2017, https://www.brainyquote.com/quotes/quotes/w/wendellber461102.html?src=t_prayer.

9   Matthew 6, The Lord's Prayer.

10   Contained in the Catholic apocrypha.

11   Proverbs 22.6, NIV.

12   Teresa of Avila, "Saint Teresa of Avila Quotes," *BrainyQuote*, accessed May 11, 2017, https://www.brainyquote.com/quotes/quotes/s/saintteres586959.html.

13   Daniel 6.10.

14   The Navigators, "The Prayer Hand," *The Navigators*, January 31, 2006. Accessed May 11, 2017, https://www.navigators.org/Tools/Discipleship%20Resources/Tools/The%20Prayer%20Hand.

CHAPTER TWO: PRAYER MAKES US SAINTS

15   Quoted in Rolheiser, Ronald, *Prayer: Our Deepest Longing,* (Franciscan Media: Cincinnati, OH, 2013), 35.

16 Lincoln, Abraham. "Abraham Lincoln Quotes," *Goodreads*, accessed May 11, 2017, http://www. goodreads.com/quotes/38057-i-have-been-driven-many-times-upon-my-knees-by.

17 Lewis, C.S., *Letters to Malcolm: Chiefly on Prayer: Reflections on the Intimate Dialogue Between Man and God*, (Houghton Mifflin Harcourt Publishing Company: New York, 1992), 69.

18 Crossan, John Dominic, *The Greatest Prayer: Rediscovering the Revolutionary Message of The Lord's Prayer*, (HarperCollins: New York, 2010), 13.

19 Kreeft, Peter, *Prayer for Beginners*, (Ignatius Press: San Francisco, 2000), 14.

20 Seaver, W.L., compiler, *Prayer: Communing With God in Everything—Collected Insights from A.W. Tozer*, (Moody Publishers: Chicago, 2016), 39.

21 Ignatius of Loyola, "Prayer for Generosity," *St. Ignatius: Selected Prayers*, accessed May 11, 2017, http://www.bc.edu/bc_org/prs/stign/prayers. html.

CHAPTER THREE: PRAYER IS NOT
AUTOMATIC, BUT IT CAN BE ORDINARY

22 Seaver, 18.

23 Leonard Sweet, in McDonald, David, ed., *The Story Lectionary*, (Portland Seminary: Portland, OR, 2017), 230.

24 Seaver, 31.

25 Lewis, 75.

26 Buechner, Frederick, *The Magnificent Defeat*, (HarperCollins: New York, 1966), 87.

27 Wright, N.T. *The Lord and His Prayer*, (Eerdmans: Grand Rapids, MI, 1996), 3.

28 Keller, Timothy, *Prayer: Experiencing Awe and Intimacy with God,* (Penguin Books: New York, 2014), 12.

29 Facebook comment by my friend, Del Belcher (https://www.facebook.com/delbelcher).

30 Ware, Kallistos, Bishop of Diokleia, *The Power of the Name: The Jesus Prayer in Orthodox Spirituality*, (Will Print: Oxford, England, 1986), 1.

31 Brother Lawrence, *The Practice of the Presence of God*, Trans. John J. Delaney, (Doubleday: New York, 1977), 55.

32 Cohen, 3.

33 Brother Lawrence, 47.

34 Kenneth W. Brewer is the Chair of the
    Department of Theology at Spring Arbor
    University in Spring Arbor, Michigan.

CHAPTER FOUR: THE MOST COMMON CAUSE
OF UNANSWERED PRAYER

35   Rolheiser, Ronald. *Prayer: Our Deepest Longing,*
     (Franciscan Media: Cincinnati, OH, 2013).

36 Thomas à Kempis, "Thomas à Kempis Quotes,"
    BrainyQuote. Accessed May 11, 2017, https://
    www.brainyquote.com/quotes/quotes/t/
    thomasakem386826.html.

37 Hybels, Bill, *Too Busy Not To Pray: Slowing Down to
    Be with God*, (InterVarsity Press: Downers Grove,
    IL, 2008), 98.

38   Ibid.

39 Athanasius, *On the Incarnation of the Word,*
    Christian Classics Ethereal Library, accessed May
    11, 2017, https://www.ccel.org/ccel/athanasius/
    incarnation.ii.html.

40   Ibid.

41   Leonard Sweet, *The Story Lectionary*, 230.

CHAPTER FIVE: WHY PRAYER DOESN'T WORK

42   Lewis, 58.

43   Seaver, 102.

44   Kreeft, Peter, *Prayer for Beginners,* (Ignatius Press: San Francisco, 2000), 14.

45   Packer, J.I. *Praying the Lord's Prayer*, (Crossway: Wheaton, IL, 2007). 13.

46   Kierkegaard, Soren, "Soren Kierkegaard Quotes," BrainyQuote, accessed May 16, 2017, https://www.brainyquote.com/quotes/quotes/s/sorenkierk152229.html.

47   O'Connor, Flannery, as quoted in Keller, *Prayer,* 11.

48   Hybels, 17.

49   Merton, Thomas, *Thoughts in Solitude,* (Farrar, Straus, and Giroux: New York, 1956).

CHAPTER SIX: STRANGE AND UNCOMFORTABLE

50   McDonald, David, *The Church Survival Guide,* (Westwinds Church: Jackson, MI, 2014), 88.

51 Martin Luther, *Luther's Works, Volume 54,* (Table Talk: Philadelphia, 1967), 37, 38. (May 18, 1532).

52 Along with Jack Deere's persuasive text, *Surprised by the Power of the Spirit.* (Zondervan: Grand Rapids, MI, 1993).

53 Wigglesworth, Smith. *AZ Quotes,* accessed May 12, 2017, http://www.azquotes.com/quote/940558.

54 Buechner, Frederick, *Goodreads,* accessed May 12, 2017, http://www.goodreads.com/quotes/38459-go-where-your-best-prayers-take-you.

55 James, William, *BrainyQuote,* accessed May 12, 2017, https://www.brainyquote.com/quotes/quotes/w/williamjam157202.html.

56 McDonald, *The Church Survival Guide,* 88.

57 McDonald, David, *The Adventure of Happiness,* (Westwinds: Jackson, MI, 2016), WHERE, 137.

58 Wigglesworth, Smith, *All Christian Quotes,* accessed May 12, 2017, http://www.allchristianquotes.org/quotes/Smith_Wigglesworth/2035/.

59 Wigglesworth, Smith, *Goodreads,* accessed May 12, 2017, http://www.goodreads.com/quotes/1024340-the-bible-is-the-word-of-god-supernatural-in-origin.

60 Pennington, Basil, *Centering Prayer*, (Doubleday: New York, 1982).

CHAPTER SEVEN: WHY WE'RE STILL SO BAD AT PRAYER

61 Wimber, John, *Prayer: Intimate Communication* (Vineyard Ministries International: Anaheim, CA, 1997), 39.

62 Ware, 2.

63 Kreeft, 18.

64 Willimon, William H. and Stanley Hauerwas, (*Lord, Teach Us: The Lord's Prayer and the Christian Life,* Abingdon Press: Nashville, 1996), 18.

65 Kreeft, 80; my paraphrase.

66 Yancey, Philip, "Philip Yancey Quotes," *BrainyQuote*, accessed May 12, 2017, https://www.brainyquote.com/quotes/quotes/p/philipyanc527062.html.

67 Wright, 21.

68 Lewis, 26-27.

69 Julian of Norwich, *Revelations of Divine Love*, (Oxford University Press: Oxford, UK, 2015).

70 St. John of the Cross, *The Dark Night of the Soul,* Edited by Halcyon Backhouse, (Hodder & Stoughton: London, UK, 1988).

CHAPTER EIGHT: WE BECOME THE ANSWER TO OUR PRAYERS

71 von Balthasar, Hans Urs, *Prayer,* Trans. Graham Harrison, (Ignatius Press: San Francisco, 1986), 26, 58.

72 Rolheiser, 54-55.

73 Augustine, "Love God and Do What You Will," *King's Meadow Study Center,* accessed May 12, 2017, https://www.kingsmeadow.com/wp/love-god-and-do-what-you-will/.

74 St. Augustine, *AZ Quotes,* accessed May 12, 2017, http://www.azquotes.com/quote/1387642.

75 Crossan, John Dominic, *The Greatest Prayer: Rediscovering the Revolutionary Message of The Lord's Prayer,* (HarperCollins: New York, 2010), 90.

76 Mother Teresa, *Goodreads,* accessed May 12, 2017, http://www.goodreads.com/quotes/719941-i-used-to-pray-that-god-would-feed-the-hungry.

77 Muller, George, "George Muller Quotes," *BrainyQuote,* accessed May 12, 2017, https://www.brainyquote.com/quotes/authors/g/george_muller.html.

78 Muller, George, "What George Mueller Can Teach Us About Prayer," *Crossway,* accessed May 12, 2017, https://www.crossway.org/blog/2015/07/what-george-mueller-can-teach-us-about-prayer/.

CHAPTER NINE: THE FAITH WEB

79 Seaver, 159.

80 Ness, Scott M., "The Faith Web: A Networking of the Body of Christ to Mitigate Relationship Voids and Strengthen the Faith Community" (2014). Doctor of Ministry. Paper 79. http://digitalcommons.georgefox.edu/dmin/79.

81 *Church Survival Guide*, 46.

82 Seaver, 48.

83 Tozer, A.W. *Goodreads*, accessed May 12, 2017, http://www.goodreads.com/quotes/700558-it-is-doubtful-whether-god-can-bless-a-man-greatly.

CHAPTER TEN: WHAT WE'RE ALLOWED TO PRAY FOR

84 Lewis, 36.

85 Berry, Wendell, "Wendell Berry Quotes," *BrainyQuote*, accessed May 12, 2017, https://www.brainyquote.com/quotes/quotes/w/wendellber461103.html.

86 Kreeft, 48.

87   Wright, 23.

88   Alfred, Lord Tennyson, *Goodreads*, accessed
     May 12, 2017, http://www.goodreads.com/
     quotes/147923-more-things-are-wrought-by-
     prayer-than-this-world-dreams.

89   That's not to suggest I don't believe in the
     supernatural—far from it—just that this
     particular combination of circumstances gave me
     confidence nothing of the sort was going on.

90   Rolheiser, 7.

91   John of the Cross, *AZ Quotes*, accessed May 12,
     2017, http://www.azquotes.com/quote/607805.

92   Eckhart, Meister, "Meister Eckhart Quotes,"
     BrainyQuote, accessed May 12, 2017, https://www.
     brainyquote.com/quotes/authors/m/meister_
     eckhart.html.

93   Eckhart, Meister, "Meister Eckhart Quotes,"
     BrainyQuote, accessed May 12, 2017, https://www.
     brainyquote.com/quotes/authors/m/meister_
     eckhart.html.

BIBLIOGRAPHY

Balthasar, Hans Urs von. *Prayer.* Trans. Graham
    Harrison. Ignatius Press: San Francisco. 1986.

BrainyQuote. http://www.brainyquote.com.

Brother Lawrence. *The Practice of the Presence of God.*
    Trans. John J. Delaney. Doubleday: New York.
    1977.

Buechner, Frederick. *The Magnificent Defeat.*
    HarperCollins: New York. 1966.

Cohen, Leonard. *Book of Mercy.* McClelland & Stewart:
    Toronto, ON. 1984.

Crossan, John Dominic. *The Greatest Prayer: Rediscovering
    the Revolutionary Message of The Lord's Prayer.*
    HarperCollins: New York. 2010.

Deere, Jack. *Surprised by the Power of the Spirit.* Zonder-
    van: Grand Rapids, MI. 1993.

Goodreads. http://www.goodreads.com/.

Higgins, John J. *Thomas Merton on Prayer.* Image Books:
    Garden City, NY. 1971.

Hybels, Bill. *Too Busy Not To Pray: Slowing Down to Be with God.* InterVarsity Press: Downers Grove, IL. 2008.

Keller, Timothy. *Prayer: Experiencing Awe and Intimacy with God.* Penguin Books: New York. 2014.

Kelly, Thomas R. *A Testament of Devotion.* HarperCollins: New York. 1992.

Kreeft, Peter. *Prayer for Beginners.* Ignatius Press: San Francisco. 2000.

Lewis, C.S. *Letters to Malcolm: Chiefly on Prayer: Reflections on the Intimate Dialogue Between Man and God.* Houghton Mifflin Harcourt Publishing Company: New York. 1992.

Luther's Works, Volume 54, Table Talk (Philadelphia: 1967), pp. 37, 38. May 18, 1532

McDonald, David. *The Adventure of Happiness.* Westwinds Church: Jackson, MI. 2016.

McDonald, David. *The Church Survival Guide.* Westwinds Church: Jackson, MI. 2014.

McDonald, David, ed. *The Story Lectionary.* Portland Seminary: Portland, OR. 2017.

Merton, Thomas. *Thoughts in Solitude.* Farrar, Straus, and Giroux: New York. 1956.

The Navigators. https://www.navigators.org/.

Packer, J.I. *Praying the Lord's Prayer.* Crossway: Wheaton, IL. 2007.

Pennington, Basil. *Centering Prayer.* Doubleday: New York. 1982.

Peterson, Eugene H. *Praying With the Psalms: A Year of Daily Prayers and Reflections on the Words of David.* HarperCollins: New York. 1993.

Piper, John. *The Pleasures of God: Meditations on God's Delight in Being God.* Multnomah Books: New York. 1991.

Rolheiser, Ronald. *Prayer: Our Deepest Longing.* Franciscan Media: Cincinnati, OH. 2013.

Seaver, W.L., compiler. *Prayer: Communing With God in Everything—Collected Insights from A.W. Tozer.* Moody Publishers: Chicago. 2016.

Seligman, Martin. *Authentic Happiness.*

St. John of the Cross. *The Dark Night of the Soul.* Edited by Halcyon Backhouse. London: Hodder & Stoughton. 1988.

Underhill, Evelyn, ed. *The Cloud of Unknowing.* Element Classics: Rockport, MA. 1997.

Ware, Kallistos, Bishop of Diokleia. *The Power of the Name: The Jesus Prayer in Orthodox Spirituality.* Will Print: Oxford, England. 1986.

Wigglesworth, Smith. *Ever Increasing Faith.* GodSounds, Inc.: Lexington, KY. 2016.

Willimon, William H. and Stanley Hauerwas. *Lord, Teach Us: The Lord's Prayer and the Christian Life.* Abingdon Press: Nashville. 1996.

Wimber, John. *Prayer: Intimate Communication.* Vineyard Ministries International: Anaheim, CA. 1997.

Wimber, John and Kevin Springer. *Power Healing.* HarperCollins: New York. 1987.

Wright, N.T. *The Lord and His Prayer.* Eerdmans: Grand Rapids, MI. 1996.

CHECK OUT THESE OTHER RESOURCES ON AMAZON:

THE ADVENTURE OF HAPPINESS: Dr. David McDonald has researched happiness extensively--the science, sociology, psychology, and philosophy. This is where all that research has lead. We are happy because of what we do and because of who we are becoming. Happiness is available to us, increasingly, as we shift from lives of passivity to activity; from thinking to doing; and from defending to iterating (what we do). We are happy not because we don't have to change, but because we can renew our minds, govern our mouths, guard our hearts, and use our legs (who we are becoming). And in all this, we are not restrained by history, association, birth, personality, or circumstance. Want to experience greater happiness? This book can help lead you in the right direction.

DOWN TO EARTH: Life often feels too hard, even purposeless, and God seems like a distant observer. The Incarnation of Christ is not just doctrine. It is earthy and it raises the train wreck of humanity to its full dignity and potential. Re-encounter Christ, and see how he validates every minute detail of your life, and how it will change because of him.

SEASONS OF CHRISTIAN SPIRITUALITY: Liturgy. It means "the work of the people." In real life, it refers to the changing face of Christian worship scripted according to theme, season, and meaning. I'm not keen on scripts, but I am especially keen on theme and meaning. So this book is about learning to live like we normally ought, governed by the driving truths of the Scriptures, the Spirit, and the season.

HEART OF GOLD: Far from the gospel of prosperity, discover how justice and mission are fed by abundance and delight. Learn how to get on your feet financially. Use your financial freedom to serve and prosper others. Cultivate a heart of gold and free yourself from the hidden alchemy transforming your heart into a heart of greed.

MONSTERS: Throughout the scriptures, diverse species of monsters appear--false gods, apocalyptic beasts, and idols--and they strike terror in the hearts of God's people. These biblical monsters bear a strong resemblance to our contemporary monsters--fear, anxiety, depression, worry. We need to know that God is with us, and that Jesus keeps the monsters away. That's what Monsters is about.

Dr. David McDonald is a pastor, teacher, and lecturer in colleges and seminaries all over the world. His work with Westwinds Community Church has been featured in *The New York Times*, *Wall Street Journal*, and *Time* magazine.

David continues to integrate spiritual truth with sharp social analysis in his private work through www.fossores.com.

David lives with his wife, Carmel, and their two children in Jackson, Michigan.

65126246R00127

Made in the USA
Lexington, KY
01 July 2017